Beans & Rice

GENERAL EDITOR
CHUCK WILLIAMS

RECIPES
JOANNE WEIR

PHOTOGRAPHY
ALLAN ROSENBERG

TIME
LIFE
BOOKS

Time-Life Books is a division of
TIME LIFE INCORPORATED

President and CEO: John M. Fahey, Jr.
President, Time-Life Books: John D. Hall

TIME-LIFE CUSTOM PUBLISHING

Vice President and Publisher: Terry Newell
Sales Director: Frances C. Mangan
Editorial Director: Robert A. Doyle

WILLIAMS-SONOMA
Founder/Vice-Chairman: Chuck Williams

WELDON OWEN INC.
President: John Owen
Publisher: Wendely Harvey
Managing Editor: Laurie Wertz
Consulting Editor: Norman Kolpas
Copy Editor: Sharon Silva
Editorial Assistant: Janique Poncelet
Design: John Bull, The Book Design Company
Production: James Obata, Stephanie Sherman,
　Mick Bagnato
Food Photographer: Allan Rosenberg
Additional Food Photography: Allen V. Lott
Primary Food & Prop Stylist: Sandra Griswold
Food Stylist: Heidi Gintner
Assistant Food Stylist: Mara Barot
Glossary Illustrations: Alice Harth

The Williams-Sonoma Kitchen Library
conceived and produced by Weldon Owen Inc.
814 Montgomery St., San Francisco, CA 94133

In collaboration with Williams-Sonoma
100 North Point, San Francisco, CA 94133

Production by Mandarin Offset, Hong Kong
Printed in China

A Note on Weights and Measures:
All recipes include customary U.S. and metric
measurements. Metric conversions are based on
a standard developed for these books and have
been rounded off. Actual weights may vary.

A Weldon Owen Production

Copyright © 1994 Weldon Owen Inc.
Reprinted in 1994
All rights reserved, including the right of
reproduction in whole or in part in any form.

Library of Congress
Cataloging-in-Publication Data:

Weir, Joanne.
　Beans & rice : recipes / Joanne Weir ;
　photography Allan Rosenberg.
　　　p.　　cm. — (Williams-Sonoma kitchen library)
　　ISBN 0-7835-0279-6
　　1. Cookery (Beans)　2. Cookery (Rice)　I. Title.
　　II. Title: Beans and rice.　　III. Series.
　TX803.B4W45　1994
　641.8'2—dc20　　　　　　　　　93-48183
　　　　　　　　　　　　　　　　　　CIP

Contents

SOUPS & SALADS 15

MAIN COURSES 51

SIDE DISHES 85

INTRODUCTION

The phrase "a hill of beans" has long been used to describe anything considered worthless. Today, however, those same words might give pause to someone concerned with good eating.

In recent years, we've discovered that such humble foods as beans and their companionable staple, rice, possess immeasurable value for a number of reasons. Both beans and rice are complex carbohydrates, a food group from which, nutritionists and doctors tell us, we should be getting the majority of our daily calories. Both ingredients contribute generous measures of fiber to our diets. Both are rich in vitamins and minerals, and when eaten together provide protein as complete as that obtained from animal sources.

While acknowledging all these attributes, this book focuses on beans and rice for much simpler reasons: They make particularly good eating and are incredibly versatile. As you look through the 45 recipes in this book, you'll find bean and rice dishes from around the world, ideal for serving at all kinds of occasions. And, as the introductory guides to kitchen equipment and basic techniques make clear, they're also exceptionally easy to cook.

I hope you'll be encouraged to start cooking them today, and to begin exploring the remarkable range of beans and rice now available in the markets. It is a selection that is growing, as the recent popularity of these ingredients leads growers and importers to make available little-known varieties or ancient strains that had been on the verge of extinction. Let this book inspire you to bring not a hill but a mountain of beans and rice to your dining table!

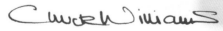

EQUIPMENT

A few basic tools serve all your needs when cooking two easy-to-prepare main ingredients

The simple array of equipment shown here reflects the utter simplicity of preparing beans and rice.

Because such dishes are generally simmered or steamed, stove-top vessels are the most essential pieces of kitchen equipment. They should be large enough to hold good-size quantities of beans or rice, both of which expand considerably as they cook. Apart from that, the usual assortment of tools helps the work go more easily, from well-calibrated spoons and cups that assure accurate measures to bowls that hold beans while they presoak to ovenproof dishes for baked preparations.

1. Food Processor
For chopping, puréeing or mixing large quantities of ingredients.

2. Stockpot
Tall, deep, large-capacity pot with close-fitting lid, for making stock or cooking large quantities of beans or rice. Select a good-quality heavy pot that absorbs and transfers heat well. Enameled steel, shown here, or anodized aluminum cleans easily and does not react with the acidity of any wine, citrus juice or tomatoes added during cooking.

3. Colander
For rinsing and sorting through beans and rice, draining beans after soaking, and draining vegetables after washing.

4. Assorted Kitchen Tools
Crockery jar holds wooden, metal and slotted spoons; wire whisk; and fine-meshed skimmer for removing froth and scum from the surface of simmering stocks and bean and rice dishes.

5. Cheesecloth & Kitchen String

Cheesecloth (muslin) and string used for making a bouquet garni—a small bag holding herbs and seasonings to be simmered in the pot and removed after cooking.

6. Ladle

For ladling stock and serving beans or rice.

7. Cheese Grater

Sturdy half-cylindrical model quickly grates hard cheeses such as Parmesan.

8. Paring Knife & Chef's Knife

Small-bladed paring knife peels vegetables and cuts up small ingredients; larger chef's knife is used for all-purpose chopping and slicing of large items or large quantities of ingredients.

9. Saucepan

For steaming rice or simmering small quantities of beans or rice. A tight-fitting lid is necessary for cooking rice.

10. Mixing Bowls

Sturdy bowls in graduated sizes for a variety of tasks ranging from mixing small amounts of dressing to soaking large quantities of beans.

11. Sieves

Fine-mesh strainer basket and smaller wire sieve for removing solids from stock, rinsing rice, or draining beans.

12. Frying Pan

Choose good-quality heavy aluminum, stainless steel, cast iron or enamel for rapid browning or frying. Sloped, shallow sides facilitate turning of ingredients and allow moisture to escape more easily for better browning.

13. Baking Dishes

Smaller oval and larger rectangular dishes for oven-baked bean or rice recipes.

14. Casserole

For use on the stove top or in the oven, large-capacity enameled metal cooking vessel with tight-fitting ovenproof lid holds baked, braised or stewed dishes.

15. Measuring Spoons

For measuring small quantities of ingredients such as herbs or salt. Select good-quality, calibrated metal spoons with deep bowls.

16. Measuring Cups

For accurate measuring of dry ingredients. Choose a set in graduated sizes. For liquids, use a heavy-duty, heat-resistant glass measuring cup.

Bean Basics

The 17 different dried beans, lentils and peas shown at right only begin to suggest the wide range of choices available at food markets, farmers' markets and health-food stores. The ever-growing interest in these foods and the contributions they make to healthful diets have helped fuel the rediscovery of many long-lost varieties.

When buying any kind of dried bean, lentil or pea, seek out a source that has a regular turnover— whether the beans are sold prepackaged in sealed plastic bags or in bulk from canisters or burlap bags. Try to inspect them before you buy, avoiding any that lack uniformity or look otherwise unusual in size, shape or color. Also check for signs of mold, which indicate that they weren't dried properly. Don't buy more than you are likely to cook within a few months; over time, beans, lentils and peas become drier still, requiring longer cooking. Store them in airtight containers at cool room temperature.

Dried beans require presoaking before cooking (see sidebar, opposite), primarily to rehydrate them. Dried lentils and peas, having thinner skins or no skins and being smaller and less dense, can be cooked without soaking. Once cooking commences, however, all of them should be brought slowly to a full boil; lentils and peas should then be boiled briefly, while beans should be boiled for 10 full minutes. (The high temperature helps neutralize the natural toxins they contain, which would otherwise cause gastric distress.) Then reduce the heat and simmer until they are tender; exact cooking times will vary with their variety, age and dryness.

Virtually all cooked dishes of beans, lentils and peas freeze and reheat very well. Store them in airtight freezer containers, labeled and dated, and use within 1 year.

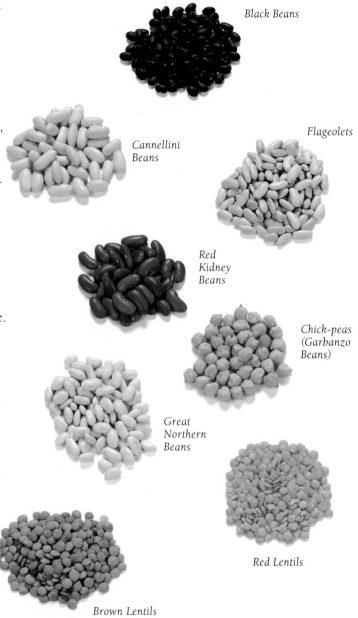

Black Beans

Flageolets

Cannellini Beans

Red Kidney Beans

Chick-peas (Garbanzo Beans)

Great Northern Beans

Red Lentils

Brown Lentils

White
Kidney
Beans

Black-eyed Peas

Pinto Beans

Yellow Split Peas

Cranberry Beans

Small White
(Navy) Beans

Adzuki Beans

Baby Lima Beans

Dried Fava
(Broad) Beans

SORTING, RINSING & SOAKING DRIED BEANS

During the drying process, beans, lentils and peas may get mixed with a few small stones or fibers. Before use, they should be carefully picked over to remove any such impurities, as well as any discolored or misshapen specimens. A thorough rinsing in a colander or sieve under cold running water will then remove any dust clinging to their surfaces.

Next, to rehydrate them and thus ensure even and thorough cooking, whole beans are usually presoaked in enough cold water to cover generously. Common wisdom has long held that the presoaking should last 8–12 hours. But new methods of drying beans now make such extended soaking unnecessary. Most beans now need only about a 3-hour soak. Or, alternatively, bring the dried beans to a simmer, cover the pot, remove it from the heat and let them soak for 1–1½ hours before draining and continuing with the recipe.

Sorting through the beans.
Spread out the beans in small batches on a platter or tray that allows you to see them clearly in a single layer. Pick out and discard any impurities or discolored or misshapen beans. Transfer the beans to a colander or sieve and rinse well under cold running water.

Soaking the beans.
Put the cleaned beans in a bowl large enough to hold them all comfortably and add enough fresh cold water to cover them generously. Leave to soak at room temperature for about 3 hours, then drain well and proceed with the recipe.

RICE BASICS

Scan your food store's shelves and you'll find a wide, sometimes bewildering array of rices for sale. For the most part, however, they break down into the few basic categories for which general cooking strategies are given below.

The seeds of a grass first domesticated in Asia more than 5,500 years ago, rice varieties generally fall into three main types, described by their size and shape: short, medium and long grain. Most rice is sold in the so-called polished form commonly known as white rice—grains from which the hulls have first been removed and then the brown coating of bran milled away, leaving just the white starchy interior. Leaving the bran intact results in more robust-tasting brown rice. The properties of each rice variety, in turn, suit it best to particular recipes: Italian Arborio rice, for example, releases so much starch into the cooking liquid that it produces the creamy sauce of a risotto, while long-grained basmati steams to form a pilaf's fragrant, fluffy grains.

Wild rice is a case unto itself. Not related to rice at all, the unpolished kernels of this wild grain native to Minnesota have a rich flavor and texture that are often compared to that of nuts.

All forms of rice, as well as wild rice, should be stored in airtight containers at cool room temperature. They will keep for up to 1 year.

Arborio Rice
Short, round, polished grains from Italy, used for making risotto. Stir with a small quantity of simmering liquid, adding more liquid only after the previous liquid is absorbed, until the grains are tender and produce a creamy sauce, 30–40 minutes.

Wild Rice
Long, unpolished wild grains. Boil in water until tender; or simmer, covered, with 3 parts liquid to 1 part rice for about 1 hour.

Long-Grain Rice
Long, polished form yields separate, fluffy grains. Simmer, covered, in 1¾ parts liquid to 1 part rice for 15 minutes, depending upon how soft or moist a result is required.

Short- or Medium-Grain Rice
Shorter, starchier polished form that sticks together when cooked. Rinse if a less sticky result is desired. Simmer, covered, in 1½ parts liquid to 1 part rice for 15–20 minutes.

Basmati Rice
Long-grained variety that cooks to form fluffy, aromatic individual grains. Simmer, covered, in 1¾ parts liquid to 1 part rice for 15 minutes, depending upon how soft or moist a result is required.

Brown Rice
Grains with their bran coating intact, yielding chewy rice with a nutlike flavor. Simmer, covered, in 2 parts liquid to 1 part rice for 45–60 minutes.

Vegetable Stock

This is a great basic stock for vegetarian cooking. It should be simmered for only 1–1½ hours to ensure a sweet fresh flavor. Any number of vegetables can be used, for a wide range of results: onions, leeks, carrots, celery, tomatoes, potatoes, mushrooms, green beans, squash, garlic, fennel, eggplant (aubergine) and cabbage, and greens such as spinach, Swiss chard and lettuce. Avoid cauliflower, Brussels sprouts, artichokes, and beets or beet greens because of their strong flavors. The trimmings can be leftover vegetable peelings, fennel stalks, mushroom and spinach stems, lettuce leaves, and the like.

10 cups (2 lb/1 kg) chopped vegetables and/or
　trimmings
1 yellow onion, coarsely chopped
1 carrot, coarsely chopped
12 parsley stems
pinch of dried or fresh thyme leaves
1 bay leaf

Place all the vegetables in a stockpot or large saucepan. Use the remaining ingredients to make a bouquet garni: Combine the parsley stems, thyme and bay leaf on a small piece of cheesecloth (muslin), bring the corners together and tie with kitchen string to form a bag. Add to the pot along with water to cover the vegetables by 2–3 inches (5–7.5 cm).

　Bring to a boil, then immediately reduce the heat so the liquid simmers gently. Simmer, uncovered, until the stock has a good aroma and flavor, 1–1½ hours. Add water to maintain the original level as necessary.

　Strain the stock through a fine-mesh sieve into a bowl and let cool. To store, transfer to a container with a tight-fitting lid and refrigerate for up to 3 days or freeze for up to 2 months.

Makes 2–3 qt (2–3 l)

Chicken Stock

Some cooks add too much water when making stock, which dilutes the flavor of the finished product. You should add water to cover the solid ingredients by no more than 2–3 inches (5–7.5 cm). Store in small plastic containers in the freezer so you always have some on hand.

5 lb (2.5 kg) chicken parts such as backs, necks
　and wings
1 yellow onion, coarsely chopped
1 carrot, coarsely chopped
12 parsley stems
pinch of dried or fresh thyme leaves
1 bay leaf

Trim away any excess fat from the chicken parts. Place the parts in a stockpot or large saucepan along with the onion and carrot. Use the remaining ingredients to make a bouquet garni: Combine the parsley stems, thyme and bay leaf on a small piece of cheesecloth (muslin), bring the corners together and tie with kitchen string to form a bag. Add to the pot along with water to cover the chicken parts by 2–3 inches (5–7.5 cm).

　Bring to a boil, then immediately reduce the heat so the liquid simmers gently. Skim off any scum that forms on the surface. Simmer, uncovered, until the stock has a good flavor and the meat has fallen from the bones, 3–4 hours. Continue to skim as necessary. Add water to maintain the original level as necessary.

　Strain the stock through a fine-mesh sieve into a bowl. Place in the refrigerator and allow to cool completely. Remove the congealed fat from the surface and discard. To store, transfer to a container with a tight-fitting lid and refrigerate for up to 3 days or freeze for up to 2 months.

Makes 2–3 qt (2–3 l)

Beef, Veal or Lamb Stock

Roasting the bones for this stock is optional. If you do roast them, the stock will have a darker color and a deeper taste. Veal breastbones offer the best flavor and ensure a fine gelatinous quality. To use them, cut completely apart between the ribs and place the ribs well spaced in a pan for roasting.

5 lb (2.5 kg) meaty beef, veal or lamb bones
1 yellow onion, coarsely chopped
1 carrot, coarsely chopped
12 parsley stems
pinch of dried or fresh thyme leaves
1 bay leaf

Position a rack in the center of an oven. Preheat the oven to 400°F (200°C).

Place the bones in a roasting pan, spacing them well apart. Bake on the center rack until russet brown, 1–2 hours.

Transfer the bones to a stockpot or large saucepan. Add the onion and carrot. Use the remaining ingredients to make a bouquet garni: Combine the parsley stems, thyme and bay leaf on a small piece of cheesecloth (muslin), bring the corners together and tie with kitchen string to form a bag. Add to the pot along with water to cover the bones by 2–3 inches (5–7.5 cm).

Place the roasting pan on the stove top and pour about 1 cup (8 fl oz/250 ml) water into it. Bring to a boil and deglaze the pan, scraping up any browned bits stuck to the bottom. Add to the stockpot.

Bring to a boil, then immediately reduce the heat so the liquid simmers gently. Skim off any scum that forms on the surface. Simmer, uncovered, until the stock has a good flavor and the meat has fallen from the bones, 4–5 hours. Continue to skim as necessary. Add water to maintain the original level as necessary.

Strain the stock through a fine-mesh sieve into a bowl. Place in the refrigerator and allow to cool completely.

Remove the congealed fat from the surface and discard. To store, transfer to a container with a tight-fitting lid and refrigerate for up to 3 days or freeze for up to 2 months.

Makes 2–3 qt (2–3 l)

Tomato Sauce

This sauce has a spicy, fresh flavor. If sweet red summer tomatoes are available, use them; otherwise, good-quality canned tomatoes will work well. The balsamic vinegar accentuates the sweetness of the sauce, and the red pepper flakes provide a perfect contrast to the sweetness. This sauce is used in several recipes in this book, and also makes a delicious sauce for pasta.

2 tablespoons extra-virgin olive oil
1 yellow onion, chopped
8 ripe tomatoes, peeled, seeded and diced, or 1 can
    (28 oz/875 g) plum (Roma) tomatoes, drained and
    chopped
½ teaspoon dried oregano
large pinch of red pepper flakes
2 tablespoons balsamic vinegar
1 tablespoon tomato paste
¼ cup (2 fl oz/60 ml) dry red wine
½ teaspoon sugar
salt and freshly ground pepper

In a large frying pan over medium heat, warm the olive oil. Add the onion and sauté, stirring, until soft, about 10 minutes.

Add the tomatoes, oregano, red pepper flakes, vinegar, tomato paste, red wine, sugar and salt and pepper to taste. Bring to a simmer and cook gently, uncovered, until the sauce thickens, about 20 minutes. Stir 2 or 3 times during cooking to prevent scorching. Remove from the heat and let cool.

Transfer the sauce to a blender or to a food processor fitted with the metal blade. Purée until smooth. Taste and adjust the seasoning with salt and pepper. Use the sauce hot or at room temperature. Store in a tightly covered container in the refrigerator for up to 3 days or in the freezer for up to 2 months.

Makes about 2 cups (16 fl oz/500 ml)

Garlic Mayonnaise

Just a few tips will make preparing mayonnaise easier. First, make sure all the ingredients are at room temperature. Begin by making an emulsion with the egg yolk, mustard and just 1 tablespoon of the oil, then add the remaining oil very slowly. Mayonnaise can also be made in a blender or in a small food processor fitted with the metal blade using this same basic method, with the motor running as the oil is added. This garlic-flavored mayonnaise, also called aioli, makes a good sauce for peppers stuffed with rice, tomatoes and corn (recipe on page 101) and a spritely yet simple dressing for warm white and green bean salad with tuna (page 16).

1 egg yolk
1 teaspoon Dijon mustard
⅓ cup (3 fl oz/80 ml) olive oil
⅓ cup (3 fl oz/80 ml) safflower or peanut oil
3 cloves garlic, finely minced
salt and freshly ground pepper
juice of ½ lemon
2 tablespoons warm water, if using for a sauce

*I*n a bowl, whisk together the egg yolk, mustard and 1 tablespoon of the olive oil until an emulsion forms. Combine the remaining olive oil and the safflower or peanut oil in a pitcher. Drop by drop, add 2–3 tablespoons of the oil to the egg yolk mixture while whisking constantly. Once the mixture has thickened, add the remaining oil in a very fine, steady stream, whisking constantly, until all of it has been incorporated.

Stir in the garlic and season to taste with salt and pepper and the lemon juice. If using the mayonnaise as a sauce, whisk in the warm water to lighten the mayonnaise and make it barely fluid.

Makes about 1 cup (8 fl oz/250 ml)

Summer Minestrone with Pesto

1 cup (7 oz/220 g) dried fava (broad)
  beans, preferably already peeled
¼ cup (2 fl oz/60 ml) plus ⅓ cup
  (3 fl oz/80 ml) extra-virgin olive oil
1 yellow onion, finely chopped
2 carrots, peeled and cut into ¼-inch
  (6-mm) dice
2 celery stalks, cut into ¼-inch
  (6-mm) dice
1 bunch Swiss chard, stemmed and
  cut into strips ½ inch (12 mm) wide
2 cups (12 oz/375 g) peeled, seeded
  and chopped tomatoes (fresh or
  canned)
7 cups (56 fl oz/1.75 l) chicken stock
  (recipe on page 11) or water
5 cloves garlic, minced
2½ cups (2½ oz/75 g) packed fresh
  basil leaves, washed and well dried
1 cup (4 oz/120 g) freshly grated
  Parmesan cheese
salt and freshly ground pepper
¼ cup (2 oz/60 g) Arborio rice

In the hot summer, Italians often serve this satisfying soup chilled. Traditionally pesto is made with pine nuts, but they have been omitted in this recipe. Spoon the pesto directly on top of the soup, or pass a small bowl at the table for guests to help themselves.

*P*ick over and discard any damaged beans or stones. Rinse the beans. Place in a bowl, add plenty of water to cover and soak for about 3 hours.

Drain the beans. If you are not using already peeled beans, bring a saucepan three-fourths full of water to a boil. Add the drained beans and boil for 5 minutes. Drain and slip off the tough skin surrounding each bean.

In a large, heavy pot over low heat, warm the ¼ cup (2 fl oz/ 60 ml) olive oil. Add the onion, carrots and celery and sauté until soft, about 15 minutes. Add the chard, tomatoes, stock or water and the beans. Bring to a boil, reduce the heat to low and simmer, uncovered, until the beans are tender, about 45 minutes.

Meanwhile, in a blender or in a food processor fitted with the metal blade, combine the garlic, basil, ½ cup (2 oz/60 g) of the cheese and the ⅓ cup (3 fl oz/80 ml) olive oil. Process until smooth. Season to taste with salt and pepper. Set aside.

Once the beans are tender, stir in the rice and simmer until the rice is completely cooked, about 20 minutes. Season with salt and pepper. Ladle into individual bowls and top each with a large spoonful of pesto. Garnish with some of the remaining ½ cup (2 oz/60 g) Parmesan. Serve immediately and pass the remaining cheese at the table.

Serves 6–8

Warm White and Green Bean Salad with Tuna

¾ cup (5 oz/155 g) dried small white
  (navy) beans
¾ lb (375 g) fresh tuna fillet or 2 cans
  (6 oz/185 g each) water-packed
  albacore tuna, drained
6 tablespoons (3 fl oz/90 ml) extra-
  virgin olive oil
5 tablespoons (2½ fl oz/75 ml) red
  wine vinegar
salt and freshly ground pepper
½ lb (250 g) green beans, trimmed
1½ cups (9 oz/280 g) cherry tomatoes,
  halved
1 cup (8 fl oz/250 ml) garlic
  mayonnaise (*recipe on page 13*)
20 fresh basil leaves

In this recipe, aioli—the Provençal garlic mayonnaise—melts over the warm beans and imparts the heady flavor of garlic.

P̄ick over and discard any damaged beans or stones. Rinse the dried beans. Place in a bowl, add plenty of water to cover and soak for about 3 hours. Drain and place in a saucepan with water to cover by 2 inches (5 cm). Bring to a boil, reduce the heat to low and simmer, uncovered, until tender, 45–60 minutes.

Meanwhile, if using fresh tuna, prepare a fire in a charcoal grill. Brush the tuna with 1 tablespoon of the olive oil. Grill, turning once, 3–4 minutes on each side for medium. Alternatively, place the oil-brushed tuna in a frying pan and panfry, turning once, 3–4 minutes on each side. Let cool.

In a small bowl, whisk together 4 tablespoons (2 fl oz/60 ml) of the vinegar, the remaining 5 tablespoons (2½ fl oz/75 ml) oil and salt and pepper to taste. Drain the white beans and place in a bowl. Add half of the dressing and toss. Cover and keep warm.

Bring a saucepan three-fourths full of water to a boil. Add salt to taste and the green beans and boil until tender but still slightly crisp, 5–8 minutes. Drain well and keep warm.

Break the fresh or canned tuna into large bite-size pieces. Toss with the remaining dressing and salt and pepper to taste. Combine the tomatoes with the remaining 1 tablespoon vinegar and salt and pepper to taste. Toss well.

Arrange the white beans, green beans, tuna and tomatoes on a platter and top with a spoonful of the mayonnaise. Garnish with the basil and serve. Pass the remaining mayonnaise.

Serves 6

White Bean Soup with Rosemary and Parmesan

1½ cups (10½ oz/330 g) dried small white (navy) beans
3 tablespoons olive oil
1 yellow onion, finely chopped
1 carrot, peeled and finely chopped
1 celery stalk, finely chopped
2 cloves garlic, minced
1 teaspoon minced fresh rosemary
7 cups (56 fl oz/1.75 l) chicken or vegetable stock *(recipes on page 11)* or water
salt and freshly ground pepper
½ cup (2 oz/60 g) freshly grated Parmesan cheese
1 tablespoon chopped fresh parsley

A sturdy soup that is a meal in itself, this is a popular dish in northern Italy, especially Tuscany, where the locals are nick-named mangiafagioli, *or "bean eaters." Feel free to substitute other dried beans such as chick-peas (garbanzo beans), white kidney beans or cannellini beans. If you like, garnish with croutons in addition to the Parmesan and parsley.*

Pick over and discard any damaged beans or stones. Rinse the beans. Place in a bowl, add plenty of water to cover and soak for about 3 hours. Drain the beans and set aside.

In a large soup pot over medium heat, warm the olive oil. Add the onion, carrot and celery and sauté, stirring, until the vegetables are soft, about 10 minutes.

Add the garlic and rosemary and continue to sauté for 3 minutes. Add the drained beans and the stock or water. Bring to a boil, reduce the heat to low and simmer gently, uncovered, until tender, 1–1½ hours. Remove from the heat and let cool slightly.

Place one-third of the bean mixture in a blender or in a food processor fitted with the metal blade. Purée until smooth. Return the purée to the soup and reheat gently. Season to taste with salt and pepper.

Ladle the soup into individual bowls. Garnish with the Parmesan cheese and parsley and serve immediately.

Serves 6

Black Bean Soup with Tomato Salsa

1¼ cups (9 oz/280 g) dried black beans
¼ cup (2 fl oz/60 ml) olive oil
1 large yellow onion, minced
3 cloves garlic, minced
1 teaspoon ground cumin
2 teaspoons chili powder
8 cups (64 fl oz/2 l) water

FOR THE SALSA:
2 tomatoes, peeled, seeded and
  chopped
¼ cup (1½ oz/45 g) minced red
  (Spanish) onion
½ fresh jalapeño pepper, seeded and
  minced
1–2 tablespoons fresh lime juice
2 tablespoons chopped fresh cilantro
  (fresh coriander)
salt and freshly ground pepper

One of the great all-American soups, this southwestern specialty can be garnished with a wide variety of choices: grated Cheddar cheese, chopped fresh cilantro, a dollop of sour cream, diced red onions, minced jalapeños or a simple squeeze of fresh lime juice.

Pick over and discard any damaged beans or stones. Rinse the beans. Place in a bowl, add plenty of water to cover and soak for about 3 hours.

Drain the beans. In a large saucepan over medium heat, warm the olive oil. Add the yellow onion and sauté until soft, about 10 minutes. Add the garlic, cumin, chili powder, drained beans and the water. Bring to a boil, reduce the heat to low and simmer gently, uncovered, until the beans are very tender and begin to fall apart, 2–3 hours.

Meanwhile, to make the salsa, stir together the tomatoes, red onion, jalapeño, lime juice, cilantro and salt and pepper to taste in a bowl. Set aside.

When the soup is ready, season to taste with salt and pepper. Ladle into individual bowls and garnish each serving with a spoonful of the salsa. Serve immediately.

Serves 6

Fresh Fava Beans with Garlic-Lemon Dressing

3½ lb (1.75 kg) fresh fava (broad) beans
  in the pod, shelled
2 tablespoons fresh lemon juice
⅓ cup (3 fl oz/80 ml) extra-virgin
  olive oil
1 clove garlic, minced
2 tablespoons chopped fresh parsley
salt and freshly ground pepper
lemon wedges

Refreshing, light and flavorful. For added color and flavor, throw in a few strips of prosciutto or poached shrimp (prawns).

Bring a pot three-fourths full of water to a boil. Add the fava beans and simmer for 20 seconds. Drain and let cool. Peel the beans and discard the peels. Place the beans in a salad bowl.

In a small bowl, whisk together the lemon juice, olive oil, garlic, parsley and salt and pepper to taste. Add to the beans and toss well.

Place on a platter and garnish with lemon wedges.

Serves 4–6

Yellow Split Pea Soup with Spiced Yogurt

1½ cups (10½ oz/330 g) yellow split
  peas
3 tablespoons butter
1 yellow onion, chopped
1 carrot, peeled and cut into ¼-inch
  (6-mm) dice
2 teaspoons grated, peeled fresh ginger
7 cups (56 fl oz/1.75 l) chicken or
  vegetable stock (*recipes on page 11*)
  or water
salt and freshly ground pepper

FOR THE GARNISH:
½ cup (4 oz/125 g) plain yogurt
⅛ teaspoon ground turmeric
⅛ teaspoon ground cumin
⅛ teaspoon ground coriander
salt and freshly ground pepper

3 tablespoons chopped fresh cilantro
  (fresh coriander)

This mildly gingery soup is best when served hot, but it is also good chilled. The distinctive yogurt topping is similar to Indian raita, a blend of yogurt and various spices.

Pick over and discard any damaged peas or stones. Rinse the peas. Drain.

In a soup pot over medium heat, melt the butter. Add the onion and carrot and sauté, stirring, until the vegetables are soft, about 10 minutes. Add the ginger and stock or water. Bring to a boil, reduce the heat to low and simmer gently until the peas are completely soft, 45–60 minutes.

Remove from the heat and let cool slightly. Working in batches, place in a food processor fitted with the metal blade or in a blender. Purée until smooth. Thin with water or stock, if necessary, to achieve the proper consistency. Return the purée to a clean pan and reheat gently to serving temperature. Season to taste with salt and pepper.

Meanwhile, to make the garnish, in a small bowl whisk together the yogurt, turmeric, cumin, ground coriander and salt and pepper to taste.

Ladle the soup into individual bowls. Drizzle with the spiced yogurt and sprinkle with the cilantro.

Serves 6

Mixed Bean Salad with Balsamic Dressing

½ cup (3½ oz/105 g) dried black beans
½ cup (3½ oz/105 g) dried black-eyed peas
½ cup (3½ oz/105 g) dried adzuki beans
¼ cup (2 fl oz/60 ml) balsamic vinegar
2 teaspoons Dijon mustard
½ cup (4 fl oz/125 ml) extra-virgin olive oil
salt and freshly ground pepper
½ lb (250 g) green beans, trimmed and cut into 1-inch (2.5-cm) lengths
1 small red (Spanish) onion, chopped
3 tablespoons chopped fresh parsley

Bursting with colors and flavors, this nutritious salad is made from a medley of beans. Hard-cooked eggs would make a nice garnish. Slices of toasted or grilled bread rubbed with garlic and doused with olive oil can be served on the side.

Pick over and discard any damaged beans or stones. Rinse the dried beans separately. Place the beans in separate bowls, add plenty of water to cover and soak for about 3 hours.

Drain the beans and place in separate saucepans with water to cover by 2 inches (5 cm). Bring to a boil, reduce the heat to low and simmer, uncovered, until the skins begin to crack and the beans are tender, about 1 hour for the black beans, 45 minutes for the black-eyed peas and 30 minutes for the adzuki beans. Drain and combine in a large bowl.

Meanwhile, in a small bowl, whisk together the vinegar, mustard, olive oil and salt and pepper to taste. Add to the warm beans, toss well and let cool.

Bring a saucepan three-fourths full of water to a boil. Add salt to taste and the green beans and boil until tender, 4–5 minutes. Drain and let cool.

Add the green beans, onion and parsley to the cooled mixed beans. Toss well and serve at room temperature or chilled.

Serves 6

Spicy Chinese Chicken and Rice Salad

6 tablespoons (3 fl oz/90 ml) soy sauce

2 tablespoons molasses

4 tablespoons (2 fl oz/60 ml) Asian sesame oil

1 chicken, about 3½ lb (1.75 kg)

¾ cup (5 oz/155 g) long-grain white rice or basmati rice

1½ cups (12 fl oz/375 ml) chicken or vegetable stock (recipes on page 11) or water

½ teaspoon salt, plus salt to taste

3 tablespoons peanut oil

¼ cup (2 fl oz/60 ml) rice vinegar

1 clove garlic, minced

1 tablespoon minced, peeled fresh ginger

½ fresh jalapeño pepper, seeded and minced

1 teaspoon sugar

freshly ground pepper

2 green (spring) onions, including tender green tops, thinly sliced

Preheat an oven to 425°F (220°C).

In a small bowl, whisk together 2 tablespoons of the soy sauce, the molasses and 2 tablespoons of the sesame oil. Place the chicken, breast side up, in a small roasting pan (on a rack, if you like) and roast for 15 minutes. Reduce the oven temperature to 375°F (190°C). Brush the chicken generously with some of the soy mixture and continue roasting, brushing with the remaining soy mixture every 10 minutes, until the chicken is crisp and shiny, about 1 hour. To test for doneness, insert an instant-read thermometer into the thickest part of the thigh away from the bone; it should register 180°F (82°C). Let cool. Bone the chicken, then cut the meat and crisp skin into long, thin strips. Set aside.

Meanwhile, if using basmati rice, rinse well and drain. In a heavy saucepan, combine the stock or water and the ½ teaspoon salt and bring to a boil. Slowly add the rice, reduce the heat to low, cover and cook, without stirring, for 20 minutes; do not remove the cover. After 20 minutes, uncover and check to see if the rice is tender. If not, re-cover and cook for a few minutes longer until the rice is done. Remove from the heat, fluff the grains with a fork and place in a bowl to cool.

In another bowl, combine the peanut oil, vinegar, the remaining 4 tablespoons soy sauce, the remaining 2 tablespoons sesame oil, the garlic, ginger, jalapeño, sugar and salt and pepper to taste. Whisk until smooth.

In a large bowl, mix together the cooled rice and dressing. Place on a platter with the chicken; garnish with the green onions.

Serves 6

Tomato Rice Soup with Garlic and Herbs

3 tablespoons olive oil
½ cup (2½ oz/75 g) garlic cloves, halved
1 small yellow onion, minced
2½ cups (15 oz/470 g) peeled, seeded and chopped tomatoes (fresh or canned)
3 cups (24 fl oz/750 ml) chicken stock (recipe on page 11)
1 cup (8 fl oz/250 ml) water
⅓ cup (2 oz/60 g) long-grain white rice
3 tablespoons mixed chopped fresh parsley and chives
1 tablespoon mixed chopped fresh oregano, thyme and/or summer savory
1 tablespoon red wine vinegar
¼ cup (2 fl oz/60 ml) fruity red wine such as Côtes du Rhône or Zinfandel
salt and freshly ground pepper

Make this light and flavorful soup at the height of summer, when tomatoes are a brilliant red and herbs bountiful. Garnish it with a touch of parsley, if you like.

In a heavy saucepan over very low heat, warm the olive oil. Add the garlic and onion and sauté, stirring, until soft, about 15 minutes. Add the tomatoes, chicken stock and the water and simmer, uncovered, for 10 minutes.

Add the rice and chopped herbs and continue to simmer, uncovered, until the rice is just cooked, 15–20 minutes longer.

Add the vinegar, red wine and salt and pepper to taste. Simmer for 2 minutes. Ladle into individual bowls and serve immediately.

Serves 6

Hummus

1 cup (7 oz/220 g) dried chick-peas
  (garbanzo beans)
juice of 2–3 lemons
½ cup (4 oz/125 g) tahini
3 tablespoons extra-virgin olive oil,
  plus additional olive oil for garnish
6 cloves garlic, minced
¼ teaspoon ground cumin
¾ teaspoon salt, plus salt to taste
paprika, minced fresh parsley, black
  olives and lemon wedges for garnish
warmed pita bread, cut into triangles

A flavorful purée made from chick-peas and tahini (toasted sesame seed paste), hummus is a popular first course in eastern Mediterranean countries. A number of garnishes are listed; you may choose to include some or all of them.

Pick over and discard any damaged chick-peas or stones. Rinse the chick-peas. Place in a bowl, add plenty of water to cover and soak for about 3 hours.

Drain the chick-peas and place in a saucepan with water to cover by 2 inches (5 cm). Bring to a boil, reduce the heat to low and simmer, uncovered, until the skins begin to crack and the chick-peas are tender, 45–60 minutes. Drain, reserving the cooking liquid. Set aside a few chick-peas to use as garnish, if you like.

In a food processor fitted with the metal blade or in a blender, combine the cooked chick-peas, juice of 2 lemons, tahini, 2 tablespoons of the reserved cooking liquid, the 3 tablespoons olive oil, garlic, cumin and the ¾ teaspoon salt. Process until a soft, creamy paste forms, adding a little more cooking liquid if needed. Taste and add more lemon juice and salt as needed.

To serve, spread the hummus on a serving plate or place in a bowl. Garnish with paprika, minced parsley, olives, lemon wedges and the reserved chick-peas. Drizzle with olive oil. Serve with warmed pita bread for dipping.

Serves 6

Wild Rice and Mushroom Soup

½ cup (3 oz/90 g) wild rice

2 cups (16 fl oz/500 ml) water, boiling

½ teaspoon salt, plus salt to taste

2 tablespoons unsalted butter

1 yellow onion, finely chopped

1 celery stalk, finely chopped

½ cup (4 fl oz/125 ml) dry white wine

¾ lb (375 g) small fresh mushrooms, sliced

4 cups (32 fl oz/1 l) chicken, beef or vegetable stock (*recipes on pages 11–12*) or water

½ cup (4 fl oz/125 ml) heavy (double) cream

freshly ground pepper

1 tablespoon chopped fresh parsley

The addition of dried mushrooms such as porcini or shiitakes will further enhance the flavor of this soup: Place ¼ ounce (7 g) dried mushrooms in a bowl, pour in boiling water to cover and let steep for 30 minutes. Drain, reserving the mushroom liquid. Chop the mushrooms and sauté them with the onion and celery. Use the reserved mushroom liquid, strained of any residue, to replace part of the stock. The result is a full-bodied soup with a pleasantly nutty taste.

Rinse the rice well and drain. Place in a heavy saucepan with the boiling water and the ½ teaspoon salt. Bring to a boil, reduce the heat to medium-low, cover and cook, without stirring, until the rice is tender and the water is absorbed, about 40 minutes. Check the pan from time to time and add a little water if the pan is dry but the rice is not yet ready. Set aside.

Meanwhile, in a soup pot over medium heat, melt the butter. Add the onion and celery and sauté, stirring, until the vegetables are soft, about 10 minutes. Add the wine and reduce over high heat until only 1–2 tablespoons remain, about 3 minutes. Add the mushrooms and sauté, stirring, until very soft, about 15 minutes.

Add the stock or water, bring to a boil, reduce the heat to low and simmer, uncovered, for 20 minutes to blend the flavors. Add the wild rice and cream and simmer for 5 minutes longer. Season to taste with salt and pepper.

Ladle into individual bowls and garnish with the parsley. Serve immediately.

Serves 6

Spring Rice Salad with Dill-Lemon Dressing

1 cup (7 oz/220 g) long-grain white rice
   or basmati rice
2½ cups (20 fl oz/625 ml) vegetable or
   chicken stock (recipes on page 11)
   or water
½ teaspoon salt, plus salt to taste
1 large fennel bulb, trimmed and cut
   lengthwise into slices ¼ inch (6 mm)
   thick
½ lb (250 g) sugar snap peas or snow
   peas (mangetouts), ends trimmed
½ lb (250 g) asparagus, trimmed and
   cut into 1-inch (2.5-cm) lengths
3–4 tablespoons fresh lemon juice
3 tablespoons chopped fresh dill
1 clove garlic, minced
½ cup (4 fl oz/125 ml) extra-virgin
   olive oil
freshly ground pepper
lemon wedges
fresh dill sprigs

This light and colorful salad is a terrific first course or side dish with grilled chicken breasts or salmon. If any of the vegetables are unavailable in the market, you can substitute green beans, zucchini (courgettes), broccoli or even fresh peas with equally delicious results.

If using basmati rice, rinse well and drain.

In a heavy saucepan, combine the stock or water and the ½ teaspoon salt and bring to a boil. Slowly add the rice, reduce the heat to low, cover and cook, without stirring, for 20 minutes; do not remove the cover. After 20 minutes, uncover and check to see if the rice is tender and the water is absorbed. If not, re-cover and cook for a few minutes longer until the rice is done. Remove from the heat, fluff the grains with a fork and place in a bowl to cool.

Bring a saucepan three-fourths full of water to a boil. Add salt to taste, the fennel and peas and blanch for 2 minutes. Using a slotted spoon, transfer the vegetables to a bowl and let cool. Add the asparagus to the same water and simmer just until tender, 3–4 minutes. Drain and let cool with the other vegetables.

In a large bowl, whisk together the lemon juice, dill, garlic, olive oil and salt and pepper to taste. Add the cooled rice and vegetables and toss together.

Place the salad on a serving platter or in a bowl. Garnish with lemon wedges and dill sprigs.

Serves 6–8

Chick-pea Salad with Olives, Green Onions and Herbs

1 cup (7 oz/220 g) dried chick-peas (garbanzo beans)

¼ cup (2 fl oz/60 ml) red wine vinegar

6 tablespoons (3 fl oz/80 ml) extra-virgin olive oil

4 cloves garlic, minced

1 tablespoon minced fresh mint

1 tablespoon minced fresh basil

1 teaspoon minced fresh thyme

1 teaspoon minced fresh rosemary

1 teaspoon minced fresh oregano

salt and freshly ground pepper

¼ cup (1 oz/30 g) Nicoise or Kalamata olives, pitted and coarsely chopped

¼ cup (1 oz/30 g) green olives, pitted and coarsely chopped

1 small bunch green (spring) onions, including 2 inches (5 cm) of the tender green tops, thinly sliced

Adapted from a dish native to the south of France, this recipe can also be made with small white (navy) beans, pinto beans, black beans, cranberry (borlotti) beans, or red or white kidney beans.

Pick over and discard any damaged chick-peas or stones. Rinse the chick-peas. Place in a bowl, add plenty of water to cover and soak for about 3 hours.

Drain the chick-peas and place in a saucepan with water to cover by 2 inches (5 cm). Bring to a boil, reduce the heat to low and simmer, uncovered, until tender, 45–60 minutes. Drain and let cool.

In a large bowl, whisk together the vinegar, olive oil, garlic, all the herbs and salt and pepper to taste. Add the cooled beans, black and green olives and onions and mix well.

Transfer to a serving bowl and serve at room temperature.

Serves 6–8

Brown Rice Tabbouleh

⅔ cup (4½ oz/140 g) brown rice

2 cups (16 fl oz/500 ml) water

½ teaspoon salt, plus salt to taste

½ cup (4 fl oz/120 ml) extra-virgin
    olive oil

4 or 5 cloves garlic, minced

1 cup (8 fl oz/250 ml) fresh lemon juice

1 bunch green (spring) onions,
    including tender green tops, cut
    crosswise into slices ¼ inch (6 mm)
    thick

2 bunches fresh parsley, chopped

4 tablespoons chopped fresh mint

4 tomatoes, cut into ¼-inch (6-mm)
    dice

1 cucumber, peeled, seeded and cut
    into ¼-inch (6-mm) dice

freshly ground pepper

romaine (cos) leaves or warmed pita
    bread

Tabbouleh, a salad eaten throughout much of the Middle East, is traditionally made with bulgur (cracked wheat), parsley and other herbs, sweet vine-ripened tomatoes and crunchy cucumbers. Here brown rice is used to make this healthful, substantial summer salad.

Rinse the rice well and drain. Place in a heavy saucepan with the water and the ½ teaspoon salt. Bring to a boil, reduce the heat to low, cover and cook, without stirring, for 45 minutes; do not remove the cover. After 45 minutes, uncover and check to see if the rice is tender and the water is absorbed. If not, re-cover and cook for a few minutes longer until the rice is done. Then uncover, drizzle with ¼ cup (2 fl oz/60 ml) of the olive oil and fluff gently with a fork to coat the grains. Let cool completely.

Place the cooled rice in the bottom of a large salad bowl. Mix together the remaining ¼ cup (2 fl oz/60 ml) olive oil, the garlic and lemon juice and drizzle over the rice. Layer the next 5 ingredients in the order given: green onions, parsley, mint, tomatoes and cucumber. Sprinkle lightly with salt and pepper and cover with plastic wrap. Refrigerate for at least 4 hours or for up to 24 hours.

Bring the salad to room temperature. Sprinkle with salt to taste and toss well. Serve with romaine leaves or warmed pita bread for scooping up bitefuls of the salad.

Serves 6–8

Black Bean Salad with Peppers and Corn

1 cup (7 oz/220 g) dried black beans
salt
kernels from 1 fresh ear of corn
½ red bell pepper (capsicum), seeded and deribbed
1 green bell pepper, seeded and deribbed
1 yellow bell pepper, seeded and deribbed
1 small red (Spanish) onion
1 clove garlic, minced
3 tablespoons chopped fresh parsley
½ cup (4 fl oz/125 ml) olive oil
4–5 tablespoons red wine vinegar
freshly ground pepper

This striking dish is perfect for summer entertaining. It can be made several hours ahead of time and is an excellent accompaniment to grilled fish, chicken or steaks.

*P*ick over and discard any damaged beans or stones. Rinse the beans. Place in a bowl, add plenty of water to cover and soak for about 3 hours.

Drain the beans and place in a saucepan with water to cover by 2 inches (5 cm). Bring to a boil, reduce the heat to low and simmer until the skins begin to crack and the beans are tender, 1–1¼ hours. Drain and let cool.

Bring a saucepan three-fourths full of water to a boil. Add salt to taste and the corn kernels and cook for 1 minute. Drain and let cool.

Cut all of the bell peppers and the red onion into ¼-inch (6-mm) dice. In a salad bowl, combine the bell peppers, onion, corn kernels, garlic and parsley and toss to mix. Add the olive oil, vinegar and salt and pepper to taste and toss again. Add the beans, toss well and serve.

Serves 6–8

Pasta and Kidney Bean Soup

1 cup (7 oz/220 g) dried white kidney
   beans or cannellini beans
2 tablespoons extra-virgin olive oil
2 oz (60 g) pancetta or bacon, minced
   (optional)
1 yellow onion, finely chopped
2 cloves garlic, minced
2½ cups (15 oz/470 g) peeled, seeded
   and chopped tomatoes (fresh or
   canned)
1 tablespoon chopped fresh sage
pinch of red pepper flakes
salt and freshly ground black pepper
4 cups (32 fl oz/1 l) chicken, beef or
   vegetable stock (recipes on pages
   11–12) or water
¾ cup (3 oz/90 g) dried semolina pasta
   such as elbow macaroni or tiny shells
freshly grated pecorino or Parmesan
   cheese

Known as pasta e fagioli *in Tuscany, this hearty first-course soup is also robust enough to be served as a main course, accompanied by crusty bread and a green salad. Substitute red kidney, pinto or cranberry (borlotti) beans, if you like.*

Pick over and discard any damaged beans or stones. Rinse the beans. Place in a bowl, add plenty of water to cover and soak for about 3 hours.

   Drain the beans and place in a saucepan with water to cover by 2 inches (5 cm). Bring to a boil, reduce the heat to low and simmer gently, uncovered, until the skins begin to crack and the beans are tender, 45–60 minutes. Drain and set aside.

   In a soup pot over medium-low heat, warm the olive oil. Add the pancetta or bacon, onion and garlic and sauté slowly, stirring, until the onions are soft, about 12 minutes. Add the tomatoes, sage, red pepper flakes and salt and black pepper to taste and simmer for 20 minutes. Add the beans and stock or water and simmer for 30 minutes longer to blend the flavors. The beans will be very tender and the soup will become stewlike.

   Add the pasta to the soup and simmer until the pasta is tender, 12–15 minutes; timing will depend upon the type of pasta.

   Ladle the soup into individual bowls. Garnish with cheese and serve immediately.

Serves 6

Warm Salad of Lentils and Walnuts

1½ cups (10½ oz/330 g) dried lentils
¼ cup (2 fl oz/60 ml) sherry vinegar
  or red wine vinegar
1 tablespoon Dijon mustard
¼ cup (2 fl oz/60 ml) olive oil
3 tablespoons walnut oil
salt and freshly ground pepper
1 cup (4 oz/125 g) walnuts
¼ lb (125 g) thinly sliced bacon or
  pancetta, cut into ½-inch (12-mm)
  dice
½ cup (1½ oz/45 g) thinly sliced green
  (spring) onions, including tender
  green tops
2 tablespoons chopped fresh parsley

An ideal first course for the winter months. Serve at room temperature or warm, garnished with a few leaves of arugula for added color.

Pick over and discard any damaged lentils or stones. Rinse the lentils. Drain and place in a saucepan with water to cover by 2 inches (5 cm). Bring to a boil, reduce the heat to low and simmer, uncovered, until tender, 15–20 minutes. Drain immediately and set aside.

Meanwhile, preheat an oven to 350°F (180°C).

In a small bowl, whisk together the vinegar, mustard, olive oil, 2 tablespoons of the walnut oil and salt and pepper to taste. Set aside.

In another small bowl, toss together the walnuts and the remaining 1 tablespoon walnut oil and season with salt and pepper. Spread out the nuts on a baking sheet and bake until lightly golden and hot, 5–8 minutes. Remove from the oven and chop coarsely. Set aside.

In a large frying pan over medium heat, fry the bacon or pancetta until lightly golden, about 8 minutes. Turn off the heat and, while the pan is still warm, add the lentils, dressing, walnuts and green onions to the bacon and drippings. Toss to mix. Season to taste with salt and pepper.

To serve, place the salad on a platter and sprinkle with the parsley.

Serves 6

Rice Salad with Scallops, Cherry Tomatoes and Saffron

1 cup (7 oz/220 g) long-grain white rice
   or basmati rice
1 bottle (12 fl oz/375 ml) clam juice
1½ cups (12 fl oz/375 ml) water
½ teaspoon salt, plus salt to taste
1 tablespoon plus ½ cup (4 fl oz/125 ml)
   extra-virgin olive oil
1 lb (500 g) scallops
freshly ground pepper
3 tablespoons white wine vinegar,
   Champagne vinegar or fresh lemon
   juice
¼ teaspoon saffron threads
1 clove garlic, minced
1 tablespoon tomato paste
2 cups (12 oz/375 g) cherry tomatoes,
   halved
3 tablespoons chopped fresh parsley
lemon wedges

Use either bay scallops or the larger sea scallops for this paella-like salad. Or feel free to substitute shrimp (prawns), squid, clams or mussels in the shell, or even chunks of swordfish.

If using basmati rice, rinse well and drain.

In a heavy saucepan, combine the clam juice, the water and the ½ teaspoon salt and bring to a boil. Slowly add the rice, reduce the heat to low, cover and cook, without stirring, for 20 minutes; do not remove the cover. After 20 minutes, uncover and check to see if the rice is tender and the water is absorbed. If not, re-cover and cook for a few minutes longer until the rice is done. Remove from the heat, fluff the grains with a fork and place in a bowl to cool.

In a frying pan over medium-high heat, warm the 1 tablespoon olive oil. If using sea scallops, add them and sauté, turning once, until cooked, about 1½ minutes on each side. If using bay scallops, sauté, turning occasionally, about 1 minute. Season to taste with salt and pepper. Set aside to cool.

In a large bowl, whisk together the vinegar or lemon juice, saffron, garlic, tomato paste and the ½ cup (4 fl oz/ 125 ml) olive oil. Add the tomatoes, 2 tablespoons of the parsley, the scallops, cooled rice and salt and pepper to taste. Toss together.

Place on a serving platter. Garnish with lemon wedges and the remaining 1 tablespoon parsley and serve.

Serves 6

Shellfish Paella

⅓ cup (3 fl oz/80 ml) olive oil
1 yellow onion, minced
1 small red bell pepper (capsicum),
  seeded, deribbed and cut into
  ½-inch (12-mm) dice
4 cloves garlic, minced
1½ cups (10½ oz/330 g) short-grain
  white rice
5 tablespoons chopped fresh parsley
½ cup (4 fl oz/125 ml) dry white wine
5 cups (40 fl oz/1.25 l) chicken stock
  (recipe on page 11)
½ cup (4 fl oz/125 ml) tomato sauce
  (recipe on page 12)
1 cup (5 oz/155 g) cut-up green beans
  (½-inch/12-mm lengths)
1 teaspoon saffron threads steeped
  in 2 teaspoons boiling water for
  1 minute
1 teaspoon salt, plus salt to taste
freshly ground pepper
1 lb (500 g) shrimp (prawns)
1½ lb (750 g) clams or mussels in
  the shell, well scrubbed (mussels
  debearded)
1 lemon, cut into wedges

A multitude of variations exist for this quintessential Spanish dish. The most common paella, made with chicken, chorizo and shellfish, requires a bit more work than this simplified version, which has as much flavor without the added effort. If possible, purchase the short-grain white rice imported from Spain marked specifically for making paella.

Preheat an oven to 325°F (165°C).

In an ovenproof paella pan or frying pan 12 inches (30 cm) in diameter, warm the olive oil over medium heat. Add the onion, bell pepper and garlic and sauté, stirring, until soft, about 10 minutes.

Add the rice and stir to coat with the oil, about 2 minutes. Sprinkle with 4 tablespoons of the parsley. Add the wine, chicken stock, tomato sauce, green beans, saffron and water, the 1 teaspoon salt and pepper to taste. Raise the heat and bring to a boil, then reduce the heat and simmer gently, uncovered, for 10 minutes. Taste and adjust the seasonings.

Discard any clams or mussels that do not close when touched. Bury the shrimp and clams or mussels in the rice and place in the oven. Bake, uncovered, until the liquid is absorbed and the rice is tender, about 20 minutes. Remove from the oven and cover with aluminum foil. Let stand for 10 minutes.

Discard any clams or mussels that did not open. To serve, garnish with the lemon wedges and the remaining 1 tablespoon parsley.

Serves 6

Rice Croquettes with Smoked Ham and Mozzarella

4 cups (32 fl oz/1 l) chicken, vegetable
  or beef stock (*recipes on pages 11–12*)
2 tablespoons unsalted butter
1½ cups (10½ oz/330 g) Arborio rice
½ cup (4 fl oz/125 ml) tomato sauce
  (*recipe on page 12*)
½ cup (2 oz/60 g) freshly grated
  Parmesan cheese
salt and freshly ground pepper
1 egg yolk, beaten
1 slice smoked ham, 3 oz (90 g), cut
  into ¼-inch (6-mm) dice
½ cup (2½ oz/75 g) fresh peas or
  thawed, frozen peas, boiled for
  1 minute and drained
3 oz (90 g) fresh or smoked mozzarella
  or Bel Paese cheese, cut into ¼-inch
  (6-mm) dice
2–3 cups (8–12 oz/250–375 g) fine
  dried bread crumbs
peanut or corn oil for deep-frying

To make a simple meal of these Italian croquettes, serve them with warm tomato sauce (recipe on page 12) and garnish with fresh basil.

*P*our the stock into a saucepan and bring to a gentle simmer.

Meanwhile, in a large, wide saucepan over medium heat, melt the butter. Add the rice and cook, stirring, for 2 minutes. Add a ladleful of the simmering stock and stir constantly. When the liquid is almost absorbed, add another ladleful. Stir steadily to keep the rice from sticking, and add more stock, a ladleful at a time, as the previous ladleful is almost absorbed. The rice is done when it is firm but tender and the center of each grain is no longer chalky, 20–25 minutes.

Remove from the heat and stir in the tomato sauce, Parmesan and salt and pepper to taste. Let cool completely, then stir in the egg yolk, mixing well. In a small bowl, toss together the ham, peas and mozzarella or Bel Paese cheese.

Scoop up 2 tablespoons of the rice mixture. Using two fingers, make an indentation in the center. Fill it with a little of the ham mixture. Finish shaping the rice by hand to make each croquette the size of a large chicken egg. Roll in bread crumbs to coat completely. Set aside.

In a saucepan, pour in oil to a depth of 3 inches (7.5 cm) and heat to 350°F (180°C), or until a bit of bread turns golden within moments of being dropped into the oil. Add the croquettes, a few at a time, and fry, turning them to cook evenly, until deeply golden, 3–5 minutes. Using a slotted spoon, transfer to paper towels to drain. Serve immediately.

Makes 24 croquettes; serves 6

Fettuccine with Cranberry Beans and Pesto

1 cup (7 oz/220 g) dried cranberry (borlotti) beans

1½ cups (1½ oz/45 g) firmly packed fresh basil leaves, plus whole basil leaves for garnish

1 cup (4 oz/125 g) freshly grated romano, pecorino or Parmesan cheese

10 tablespoons (5 fl oz/150 ml) extra-virgin olive oil

1 large yellow onion, chopped

4 cloves garlic, minced

2 cups (16 fl oz/500 ml) chicken or vegetable stock (recipes on page 11) or water

1 lb (500 g) dried semolina fettuccine

½ cup (2½ oz/75 g) toasted pine nuts (see glossary, page 106)

salt and freshly ground pepper

Feel free to substitute other beans in this recipe: red or white kidney beans, cannellini beans, chick-peas, small white (navy) beans or black-eyed peas. Or try using a different pasta.

*P*ick over and discard any damaged beans or stones. Rinse the beans. Place in a bowl, add plenty of water to cover and soak for about 3 hours.

Drain the beans and place in a saucepan with water to cover by 2 inches (5 cm). Bring to a boil, reduce the heat to low and simmer, uncovered, until completely tender, 40–50 minutes. Drain and set aside.

In a blender or in a food processor fitted with the metal blade, combine the 1½ cups (1½ oz/45 g) basil, the cheese and 6 tablespoons (3 fl oz/90 ml) of the olive oil. Process until smooth. Set aside.

In a large frying pan over medium heat, warm the remaining 4 tablespoons (2 fl oz/60 ml) olive oil. Add the onion and garlic and sauté, stirring, until soft, about 10 minutes. Add the stock or water and the beans, bring to a boil, reduce the heat to low and simmer, uncovered, until the stock is reduced by one-fourth, 5–10 minutes.

Meanwhile, bring a large pot three-fourths full of water to a boil. Add salt to taste and the fettuccine and cook until al dente, 9–12 minutes; refer to package directions for timing. Drain and place in a warmed serving bowl.

Add the bean mixture, basil mixture, pine nuts and salt and pepper to taste. Toss well. Garnish with basil leaves and serve.

Serves 6

Cassoulet Made Easy

2¼ cups (1 lb/500 g) dried Great
  Northern beans or flageolet beans
1 yellow onion, stuck with 6 whole
  cloves
¾ lb (375 g) thickly sliced bacon, cut
  into ¼-inch (6-mm) dice
2 lb (1 kg) lamb cut from leg, in one
  piece
2 lb (1 kg) pork loin, in one piece
salt and freshly ground pepper
1 lb (500 g) Toulouse or other high-
  quality pork-and-garlic sausages
8 cloves garlic, minced
6 fresh parsley stems
½ teaspoon fresh or dried thyme leaves
1 bay leaf
2 tablespoons tomato paste
¾ teaspoon ground allspice
1 cup (4 oz/125 g) fine dried bread
  crumbs

Pick over and discard any damaged beans or stones. Rinse the beans. Place in a bowl, add plenty of water to cover and soak for about 3 hours. Drain the beans and place in a saucepan with the onion and water to cover by 2 inches (5 cm). Simmer uncovered until tender, 40–50 minutes. Drain, reserving the liquid.

Preheat an oven to 350°F (180°C). In a large, heavy ovenproof pan over low heat, fry the bacon until crisp, about 5 minutes. Using a slotted spoon, transfer to a plate; reserve the drippings in the pan.

Season the lamb and pork with salt and pepper; place in the pan. Roast, basting with the bacon drippings, until just tender, about 1¼ hours. Let cool and cut into 1-inch (2.5-cm) cubes. Leave the oven set at 350°F (180°C).

Meanwhile, prick the sausages all over with a fork. Place in a saucepan, add water to cover generously and simmer over low heat until almost cooked, 12–15 minutes. Cool and cut on the diagonal into slices ½ inch (12 mm) thick.

Place one-third of the beans on the bottom of the pan in which the meats were cooked (or in a large casserole). Sprinkle with half of the bacon, garlic, meat, sausage and salt and pepper to taste. Assemble a bouquet garni: Combine the parsley stems, thyme and bay leaf on a small piece of cheesecloth (muslin) and tie with kitchen string. Add to the pan. Repeat the layers, using half of the remaining beans and all of the bacon, garlic, meats and sausage. Top with the remaining beans.

In a bowl, stir together the tomato paste, allspice, 1 teaspoon salt and 2 cups (16 fl oz/500 ml) of the bean liquid; pour into the pan. (The liquid should reach just below the level of the beans; add more liquid as needed.) Bake for 1 hour. Top with the bread crumbs and continue to bake until golden, about 1 hour longer. Discard the bouquet garni and serve.

Serves 8–10

Ragout of Lentils, Turkey Meatballs and Mint

1 lb (500 g) ground (minced) turkey
1 cup (2 oz/60 g) fresh bread crumbs
4 cloves garlic, minced
8 tablespoons (¾ oz/20 g) chopped fresh mint
2 tablespoons chopped fresh parsley
1 teaspoon paprika
¾ teaspoon ground cumin
½ teaspoon ground cloves
¼ teaspoon cayenne pepper
¾ teaspoon salt, plus salt to taste
½ teaspoon freshly ground black pepper, plus pepper to taste
1 cup (7 oz/220 g) dried brown lentils
¼ cup (2 fl oz/60 ml) extra-virgin olive oil
1 small yellow onion, cut into ¼-inch (6-mm) dice
1 small carrot, peeled and cut into ¼-inch (6-mm) dice
1 can (14 oz/440 g) plum (Roma) tomatoes, drained, with juices reserved
4 cups (32 fl oz/1 l) chicken stock *(recipe on page 11)*

A little restaurant in Nice, in the south of France, makes a fantastic version of this stew with ground lamb. Ground chicken or beef yields equally delicious results.

*P*reheat an oven to 350°F (180°C).

In a bowl, combine the turkey, bread crumbs, half of the garlic, 3 tablespoons of the mint, the parsley, paprika, cumin, cloves, cayenne pepper, the ¾ teaspoon salt and the ½ teaspoon black pepper. Mix well. Divide the mixture into 24 equal portions and form each portion into a ball. Place on a baking sheet and bake for 10 minutes. Remove from the oven and set aside.

Meanwhile, remove and discard any damaged lentils or stones. Rinse the lentils. Set aside.

In a large sauté pan over medium heat, warm the olive oil. Add the onion, carrot and the remaining garlic and sauté, stirring, until the onion is soft, about 10 minutes. Add the lentils, 1 cup (8 fl oz/250 ml) of the reserved tomato juice and the chicken stock and simmer gently, uncovered, until the lentils are tender, about 20 minutes longer.

Chop enough of the tomatoes to measure 1 cup (6 oz/185 g); reserve the remaining tomatoes for another use. Add the meatballs and chopped tomatoes to the lentils and simmer for 15 minutes to blend the flavors and finish cooking the meatballs. Season to taste with salt and black pepper.

Ladle into bowls, garnish with the remaining 5 tablespoons mint and serve.

Serves 6

Mexican Layered Tortillas and Pinto Beans

¾ cup (5 oz/155 g) dried pinto beans
  or red kidney beans
2 yellow onions, chopped
3 cloves garlic, minced
2 small green bell peppers (capsicums),
  seeded, deribbed and chopped
1 can (28 oz/875 g) plum (Roma)
  tomatoes, drained, with juices
  reserved, and chopped
¼–½ teaspoon cayenne pepper,
  optional
6 tablespoons (1 oz/30 g) chili powder
1 tablespoon ground cumin
salt and freshly ground black pepper
8 corn tortillas, each 6 inches (15 cm)
  in diameter
2 cups (8 oz/250 g) coarsely grated
  Cheddar or Monterey jack cheese
2 cups (4 oz/125 g) coarsely chopped
  lettuce
2 tomatoes, coarsely chopped

Many thanks go to Nancy Gokey, a well-seasoned New England cook, for providing this tasty dish. A wonderful garnish is a dollop of guacamole or sour cream mixed with chopped green (spring) onions.

Pick over and discard any damaged beans or stones. Rinse the beans. Place in a bowl, add plenty of water to cover and soak for about 3 hours.

Drain the beans and place in a saucepan with water to cover by 2 inches (5 cm). Bring to a boil, reduce the heat to low and simmer, uncovered, until the skins begin to crack and the beans are tender, 45–60 minutes. Drain.

In a large frying pan, combine the beans, onions, garlic, bell peppers, canned tomatoes and their juices, cayenne pepper (if desired), chili powder, cumin and salt and black pepper to taste. Bring to a simmer and cook, stirring occasionally, for 20 minutes.

Meanwhile, preheat an oven to 350°F (180°C).

Spread one-third of the bean mixture in a 9-by-13-inch (23-by-33-cm) baking dish. Top with 4 of the tortillas, overlapping evenly, and 1 cup (4 oz/125 g) of the cheese. Repeat the layers, using half of the remaining bean mixture and all of the tortillas and cheese. Top with the remaining bean mixture. Cover with aluminum foil and bake until the edges are bubbling, about 35 minutes.

Strew the lettuce and fresh tomatoes evenly over the top and serve immediately.

Serves 6

Chick-pea and Sausage Casserole

2 cups (14 oz/440 g) dried chick-peas
   (garbanzo beans)
¼ teaspoon ground cloves
¼ teaspoon ground cinnamon
6 parsley stems
pinch of thyme
1 bay leaf
¼ cup (2 fl oz/60 ml) extra-virgin
   olive oil
3 spicy pork sausages, about ¾ lb
   (375 g) total weight
1 yellow onion, minced
3 cloves garlic, minced
salt and freshly ground pepper
½ cup (2 oz/60 g) coarsely grated sharp
   Cheddar cheese

Serve this hearty dish for a fall or winter Sunday-night supper with crusty whole-grain bread, a garden salad and robust red wine.

Pick over and discard any damaged chick-peas or stones. Rinse the chick-peas. Place in a bowl, add plenty of water to cover and soak for about 3 hours.

Drain the chick-peas and place in a saucepan with the cloves, cinnamon and water to cover by 2 inches (5 cm). Assemble a bouquet garni: Combine the parsley stems, thyme and bay leaf on a small piece of cheesecloth (muslin), bring the corners together and tie with kitchen string. Add to the pan, bring to a boil, reduce the heat and simmer, uncovered, until the chick-peas are completely tender, 50–60 minutes. Set aside.

In a large, heavy shallow flameproof pan over medium heat, warm the olive oil. Prick the sausages in several places. Add to the pan along with the onion and garlic and sauté until the onion is soft, about 10 minutes. Add the chick-peas and their liquid, cover and simmer for about 20 minutes longer. Uncover and simmer slowly for another 20 minutes until the sausages are fully cooked. Add water if the chick-peas begin to dry out. Season to taste with salt and pepper. Discard the bouquet garni.

Preheat a broiler (griller).

Remove the sausages and cut on the diagonal into thin slices. Return the sausages to the pan and stir well. Top with the cheese and slip under the broiler. Broil (grill) until golden, 1–2 minutes. Serve immediately directly from the pan.

Serves 6

Brown Rice Vegetable Loaf with Yogurt Sauce

¾ cup (5 oz/155 g) brown rice
2 cups (16 fl oz/500 ml) water
½ teaspoon salt, plus salt to taste
3 tablespoons olive oil
1 bunch green (spring) onions,
   including tender green tops, thinly
   sliced
1 cup (3 oz/90 g) finely chopped fresh
   mushrooms
2 zucchini (courgettes), coarsely grated,
   drained for 30 minutes and squeezed
   dry
2 carrots, peeled and coarsely grated
½ cup (2½ oz/75 g) toasted pine nuts
   (*see glossary, page 106*)
4 tablespoons chopped fresh parsley
½ cup (2½ oz/75 g) crumbled feta
   cheese
2 eggs, lightly beaten
freshly ground pepper
1 cup (8 oz/250 g) plain yogurt
1½ tablespoons chopped fresh mint
1 clove garlic, minced

This recipe is also quite good made with a combination of short-grain white rice and wild rice. A few mint leaves make a nice garnish.

Rinse the rice well and drain. Place in a heavy saucepan with the water and the ½ teaspoon salt. Bring to a boil, reduce the heat to low, cover and cook, without stirring, for 45 minutes; do not remove the cover. After 45 minutes, uncover and check to see if the rice is tender and the water is absorbed. If not, re-cover and cook for a few minutes longer until the rice is done. Fluff the grains with a fork and let cool.

Meanwhile, preheat an oven to 375°F (190°C).

In a frying pan over medium heat, warm the olive oil. Add the onions and sauté, stirring, until soft, about 7 minutes. Add the mushrooms and sauté until their released liquid evaporates, 3–5 minutes. Transfer the onions and mushrooms to a large bowl; let cool. Add the cooked rice, zucchini, carrots, pine nuts, parsley, cheese, eggs and salt and pepper to taste. Mix well.

Oil a 5-by-9-by-3-inch (13-by-23-by-7.5-cm) loaf pan and line the bottom and sides with parchment paper. Transfer the rice mixture to the prepared pan and cover with aluminum foil. Place the loaf pan in a baking pan and pour in hot water to reach halfway up the sides of the loaf pan. Bake until set, 50–60 minutes. Let cool for 20 minutes, then unmold onto a platter.

In a small bowl, whisk together the yogurt, mint, garlic and salt and pepper to taste. Using a serrated knife, cut the loaf into slices ¾ inch (2 cm) thick. Serve hot with the yogurt sauce.

Serves 6

Spiced Rice, Red Lentils and Smoked Fish

¾ cup (5 oz/155 g) basmati rice
1½ cups (12 fl oz/375 ml) water
½ teaspoon salt, plus salt to taste
¾ cup (5 oz/155 g) dried red lentils
2 tablespoons olive oil
1 yellow onion, minced
1 lb (500 g) smoked fish fillets, flaked
3 hard-cooked eggs, chopped
¾ cup (6 fl oz/180 ml) heavy (double)
  cream
1 teaspoon grated, peeled fresh ginger
1 teaspoon curry powder
¼ teaspoon ground nutmeg
2 tablespoons chopped fresh parsley
1 tablespoon fresh lemon juice
cayenne pepper
1 lemon, cut into wedges
2 tablespoons chopped green (spring)
  onions

Known as kedgeree, this traditional English breakfast dish originated in India. Usually it is made with smoked haddock or finnan haddie, but fresh cod or snapper fillets can also be used. If using fresh fish, poach or steam it first, then let cool before flaking.

Rinse the rice well and drain. In a heavy saucepan, bring the water and the ½ teaspoon salt to a boil. Slowly add the rice, reduce the heat to low, cover and cook, without stirring, for 20 minutes. After 20 minutes, uncover and check to see if the rice is tender. If not, re-cover and cook for a few minutes longer until the rice is done. Fluff the grains with a fork and let cool.

Meanwhile, pick over and discard any damaged lentils and stones. Rinse the lentils. Place in a saucepan with water to cover by 2 inches (5 cm). Bring to a boil, reduce the heat to low and simmer, uncovered, until the lentils are done, about 15 minutes. Drain immediately and let cool.

In a frying pan over medium heat, warm the olive oil. Add the yellow onion and sauté until soft, about 10 minutes. Transfer to a large bowl and add the rice, lentils, fish, eggs, cream, ginger, curry powder, nutmeg, parsley, lemon juice and salt and cayenne pepper to taste. Mix well and transfer to the top pan of a double boiler placed over (not touching) simmering water, or to a heatproof bowl placed in the top of a pan over (not touching) simmering water. Heat to serving temperature.

Transfer to a serving dish. Garnish with the lemon wedges and green onions.

Serves 6

Lamb, Barley and White Bean Stew

¾ cup (5 oz/155 g) dried small white (navy) beans
1½ lb (750 g) well-marbled boneless lamb stew meat, trimmed and cut into 1-inch (2.5-cm) cubes
2 tablespoons all-purpose (plain) flour
3 tablespoons olive oil
½ teaspoon chopped fresh rosemary
½ teaspoon chopped fresh thyme
2 bay leaves
3 cloves garlic, minced
6 cups (48 fl oz/1.5 l) lamb, beef or veal stock (recipe on page 12)
18 pearl onions
6 carrots, peeled and cut into 1½-inch (4-cm) lengths
¼ cup (2 oz/60 g) pearl barley
1 lb (500 g) red potatoes, unpeeled and quartered
1 cup (5 oz/155 g) fresh peas or thawed, frozen peas
salt and freshly ground pepper

This hearty winter stew hints at spring with the finishing touch of peas. But any vegetables can be added—turnips, celery, zucchini (courgettes), mushrooms—depending upon the season. Serve with flaky biscuits or whole-wheat (wholemeal) muffins.

Pick over and discard any damaged beans or stones. Rinse the beans. Place in a bowl, add plenty of water to cover and soak for about 3 hours. Drain and set aside.

Coat the lamb cubes with the flour, shaking off any excess. In a large, heavy pan over medium-high heat, warm the olive oil. Add the lamb and brown well on all sides, 10–15 minutes. Add the rosemary, thyme, bay leaves, garlic, beans and stock. Bring to a boil, reduce the heat to low, cover and simmer for 1 hour.

Meanwhile, bring a saucepan three-fourths full of water to a boil. Add the pearl onions and simmer for 45 seconds. Drain, cool and, using a knife, peel off the skins.

Add the onions, carrots and barley to the stew and simmer for 30 minutes longer. Add the potatoes and simmer until the potatoes are tender, 30 minutes longer. Add the peas and simmer for 5 minutes longer. Season to taste with salt and pepper.

Ladle into individual bowls and serve immediately.

Serves 6–8

Beef-and-Rice Cabbage Rolls

1 head green cabbage, 2–3 lb (1–1.5 kg)
1½ cups (12 fl oz/375 ml) water
½ teaspoon salt, plus salt to taste
¾ cup (5 oz/155 g) short-grain white
   rice
2 tablespoons olive oil
1 small yellow onion, finely chopped
1 lb (500 g) ground (minced) beef
2 tablespoons chopped fresh parsley,
   plus parsley leaves for garnish
freshly ground pepper
2 cups (16 fl oz/500 ml) tomato sauce
   (recipe on page 12)

These can also be made with ground veal, lamb, turkey or chicken.

*F*ill a large pot three-fourths full of water and bring to a boil. Core the cabbage deeply. Immerse the cabbage in the water and cook, turning occasionally, until the leaves are translucent, about 20 minutes. Lift out the cabbage and, when cool enough to handle, remove the soft outer leaves. When you reach leaves that are still firm, return the cabbage to the boiling water and repeat the cooking and removing of the leaves. You will need 18 leaves in all. Trim each stem even with the leaf bottom.

In a heavy saucepan, combine the water and the ½ teaspoon salt and bring to a boil. Slowly add the rice, reduce the heat to low, cover and cook, without stirring, for 20 minutes; do not remove the cover. After 20 minutes, uncover and check to see if the rice is tender and the water is absorbed. If not, re-cover and cook for a few minutes longer until the rice is done.

In a frying pan over medium heat, warm the olive oil. Add the onion and sauté, stirring, until soft, about 10 minutes. Transfer the onion to a large bowl and add the rice, beef, chopped parsley and salt and pepper to taste. Mix well.

Preheat an oven to 350°F (180°C).

Place 2–3 tablespoons filling at the stem end of each cabbage leaf. Fold in the sides of the leaf and then roll up from the stem end to enclose the filling. Place the rolls, seam side down, in a 9-by-13-inch (23-by-33-cm) baking dish. Pour the tomato sauce on top and cover with aluminum foil. Bake until the leaves are tender, 1–1¼ hours. Garnish with parsley leaves and serve.

Serves 6

Three-Bean Vegetarian Chili

¾ cup (5 oz/155 g) dried pinto beans

¾ cup (5 oz/155 g) dried red kidney beans

¾ cup (5 oz/155 g) dried black beans

⅓ cup (3 fl oz/80 ml) olive oil

3 yellow onions, chopped

2 or 3 fresh serrano or jalapeño peppers, seeded (if desired) and minced

6 large cloves garlic, minced

6 tablespoons (1 oz/30 g) chili powder

2½ tablespoons ground cumin

¼ teaspoon cayenne pepper

¾ teaspoon dried oregano

2 cans (28 oz/875 g each) crushed plum (Roma) tomatoes

salt and freshly ground black pepper

This chili is versatile: Try serving it warm as an appetizer dip with tortilla chips or as a filling for burritos. Virtually any dried beans can be substituted for the beans given here. Monterey jack cheese, sour cream and chopped fresh cilantro (fresh coriander) would make good garnishes.

Pick over and discard any damaged beans or stones. Rinse the beans. Place in a bowl, add plenty of water to cover and soak for about 3 hours. Drain the beans and set aside.

In a large, heavy saucepan over low heat, warm the olive oil. Add the onions and chili peppers and sauté, stirring, until the onions are soft, about 10 minutes. Add the garlic, chili powder, cumin, cayenne and oregano and sauté, stirring, for 2 minutes. Add the beans, tomatoes and water to cover by 3 inches (7.5 cm). Bring to a boil, reduce the heat to low and simmer, uncovered, until the beans are very tender and begin to fall apart, 2½–3 hours; add water if the beans begin to dry out but are not yet cooked.

Season to taste with salt and black pepper. Ladle into individual bowls and serve.

Serves 6

Asian Fried Brown Rice with Shrimp, Peas and Sprouts

1 cup (7 oz/220 g) brown rice
2¼ cups (18 fl oz/560 ml) water
½ teaspoon salt, plus salt to taste
peanut oil for frying
2 eggs, lightly beaten
4 green (spring) onions, including
   tender green tops, thinly sliced
¾ cup (4 oz/125 g) fresh peas or
   thawed, frozen peas
½ cup (3 oz/90 g) diced cooked pork
   roast or ham
½ cup (3 oz/90 g) diced cooked shrimp
   (prawns)
2 tablespoons soy sauce
½ cup (2 oz/60 g) fresh bean sprouts
3 tablespoons fresh cilantro (fresh
   coriander) leaves

Fried rice is an ideal way to use up leftover meats and vegetables. Chicken, snow peas (mangetouts) and slivered almonds make particularly good additions. This version is made with brown rice, but feel free to use the traditional white rice.

Rinse the rice well and drain. Place in a heavy saucepan with the water and the ½ teaspoon salt. Bring to a boil, reduce the heat to low, cover and cook, without stirring, for 45 minutes; do not remove the cover. After 45 minutes, uncover and check to see if the rice is tender and the water is absorbed. If not, re-cover and cook for a few minutes longer until the rice is done. Remove from the heat, fluff the grains with a fork and let cool completely.

In a large frying pan or a wok over medium-high heat, warm 1½ teaspoons peanut oil. Pour in the eggs to form a thin sheet and cook, without stirring, until they are set, 2–3 minutes. Slide the eggs out of the pan onto a cutting surface. Slice into thin strips and reserve.

Add 1½ tablespoons peanut oil to the pan over high heat. Add the green onions and stir and toss for 30 seconds. Add the peas, pork and shrimp and stir and toss for 30 seconds. Add the rice, sprinkle with the soy sauce and continue to stir and toss for 30 seconds. Add the bean sprouts and reserved egg strips and stir and toss for 30 seconds.

Transfer to a warmed platter, garnish with the cilantro and serve immediately.

Serves 4–6

Cornish Game Hens with Wild Rice and Sausage Stuffing

½ cup (3 oz/90 g) wild rice

2 cups (16 fl oz/500 ml) water, boiling

½ teaspoon salt, plus salt to taste

3 tablespoons unsalted butter, plus
  2 tablespoons melted

1 small yellow onion, minced

1 celery stalk, cut into ¼-inch (6-mm)
  dice

½ lb (250 g) sausage meat of your
  choice, crumbled

1 cup (3 oz/90 g) chopped fresh
  mushrooms

½ teaspoon dried thyme

freshly ground pepper

6 Cornish game hens

1 cup (8 fl oz/250 ml) chicken stock
  (recipe on page 11)

Rinse the rice well and drain. Place in a heavy saucepan and add the boiling water and the ½ teaspoon salt. Bring to a boil, reduce the heat to medium-low, cover and cook, without stirring, until the rice is tender and the water is absorbed, about 40 minutes. Check the pan from time to time and add a little water if the pan is dry but the rice is not yet ready. Let cool.

Preheat an oven to 400°F (200°C).

In a large frying pan over medium heat, melt the 3 tablespoons butter. Add the onion and celery and sauté until soft, about 15 minutes. Add the sausage meat and sauté for 10 minutes. Add the mushrooms and thyme and sauté until the released mushroom liquid evaporates, 3–5 minutes. Remove from the heat. Add the wild rice and salt and pepper to taste; mix well.

Stuff the hen cavities with the rice mixture and truss closed. Place in a baking pan (on a rack, if you like). Brush the melted butter on the hens. Sprinkle with salt and pepper. Bake for 15 minutes. Reduce the heat to 325°F (165°C) and continue to bake, basting with ½ cup (4 fl oz/125 ml) of the stock, until golden and cooked through, 40–45 minutes longer.

Transfer the hens to a platter; keep warm. Strain and degrease the pan juices and pour into a small saucepan. Boil over high heat until reduced by one-fourth. Add the remaining stock to the baking pan and place over medium heat, scraping up any browned bits, until reduced by half. Strain into the saucepan.

Place the hens on individual plates. Pour the sauce into a serving bowl and pass at the table.

Serves 6

Red Beans and Rice, Southern Style

1¼ cups (9 oz/280 g) dried pinto beans
  or red kidney beans
1 small ham hock, ½ lb (250 g)
2 tablespoons olive oil
1 yellow onion, chopped
3 cloves garlic, minced
2 small red bell peppers (capsicums),
  seeded, deribbed and cut into ¼-inch
  (6-mm) dice
4 tablespoons chopped fresh parsley
2 cups (16 fl oz/500 ml) tomato sauce
  (*recipe on page 12*)
2–3 teaspoons hot-pepper sauce such
  as Tabasco
salt to taste, plus ½ teaspoon salt
freshly ground pepper
1 cup (7 oz/220 g) basmati rice
2 cups (16 fl oz/500 ml) water

The combination of rice and beans has long been a staple in the southern United States, especially in Louisiana.

*P*ick over and discard any damaged beans or stones. Rinse the beans. Place in a bowl, add plenty of water to cover and soak for about 3 hours.

Drain the beans and place in a saucepan with the ham hock and water to cover by 2 inches (5 cm). Bring to a boil, reduce the heat to low and simmer, uncovered, until the beans are tender and the skins begin to crack, about 45 minutes.

In a frying pan over medium heat, warm the olive oil. Add the onion, garlic and half of the diced bell peppers and sauté, stirring, until soft, about 10 minutes. Add the onion mixture to the beans, along with the parsley, tomato sauce, hot-pepper sauce and salt and pepper to taste. Simmer gently until thick, about 2 hours. Remove the ham hock (cut the meat from the bone and reserve for another use).

About 30 minutes before the beans are ready, rinse the rice well and drain. In a heavy saucepan, bring the water and the ½ teaspoon salt to a boil. Slowly add the rice, cover, reduce the heat to low and cook, without stirring, for 20 minutes; do not remove the cover. After 20 minutes, uncover and check to see if the rice is tender and the water is absorbed. If not, re-cover and cook for a few minutes longer until the rice is done.

Spoon the rice into individual bowls. Top with the beans, garnish with the remaining bell peppers and serve.

Serves 6

B-
needs fresh
artichokes

Risotto with Artichokes and Parmesan Cheese

juice of 1 lemon

4 large artichokes or 20 small artichokes

2 tablespoons extra-virgin olive oil

1 very small yellow onion, minced

2 cloves garlic, minced

½ cup (¾ oz/20 g) chopped fresh parsley

2½ cups (20 fl oz/625 ml) water

salt

freshly ground pepper

3 cups (24 fl oz/750 ml) chicken stock (recipe on page 11)

1½ cups (10½ oz/330 g) Arborio rice

½ cup (2 oz/60 g) freshly grated Parmesan cheese

1 lemon, cut into wedges (optional)

Use Arborio rice (or other short-grain varieties) imported from Italy to make this dish, as it results in a particularly creamy finish.

*H*ave ready a large bowl of water to which you have added half of the lemon juice. Remove the tough outer leaves of the artichokes. Trim off the stems and the prickly leaf points. If using large artichokes, cut in half lengthwise, then scoop out the prickly chokes and discard. Cut the artichokes into thin slices lengthwise. As each is cut, place in the bowl.

In a deep frying pan over medium heat, warm the olive oil. Add the onion and sauté until soft, about 10 minutes. Add the garlic and half of the parsley and sauté for 2 minutes. Drain the artichokes and add to the pan along with ½ cup (4 fl oz/125 ml) of the water and a large pinch of salt. Cover and cook over medium heat until the liquid evaporates, about 25 minutes.

Meanwhile, combine the stock and the remaining 2 cups (16 fl oz/500 ml) water in a saucepan; bring to a gentle simmer.

Uncover the artichokes, add the rice and stir for 2 minutes. Add a ladleful of the simmering stock-water mixture and stir constantly over medium heat. When the liquid is almost absorbed, add another ladleful. Stir steadily to keep the rice from sticking and add more liquid, a ladleful at a time, as the previous ladleful is almost absorbed. The risotto is done when it is firm but tender and the center of each grain is no longer chalky, 20–25 minutes.

Remove from the heat and stir in the Parmesan and the remaining parsley and lemon juice. Season to taste with salt and pepper. Transfer to a warmed serving dish and serve with lemon wedges, if you like.

Serves 6

Wild Rice and Blue Cheese Skillet Soufflé

¼ cup (1½ oz/45 g) wild rice

1 cup (8 fl oz/250 ml) water, boiling

½ teaspoon salt, plus salt to taste

2 tablespoons milk or cream

3 oz (90 g) blue cheese such as Maytag, Roquefort or Gorgonzola, crumbled

6 eggs, lightly beaten

3 tablespoons olive oil

1 yellow onion, chopped

2 cloves garlic, minced

¾ lb (375 g) spinach, carefully washed, well dried and coarsely chopped

freshly ground pepper

6 tablespoons (1½ oz/45 g) freshly grated Parmesan cheese

This easy-to-make soufflé differs from a traditional soufflé in that the eggs are not separated and it is baked in a frying pan rather than a straight-sided soufflé dish. Serve it for breakfast, lunch or a light dinner main course.

Rinse the rice well and drain. Place in a saucepan and add the boiling water and the ½ teaspoon salt. Bring to a boil, reduce the heat to medium-low, cover and cook, without stirring, until the rice is tender, about 40 minutes. Check the pan from time to time and add a little water if the pan is dry but the rice is not yet ready. Fluff the grains with a fork and let cool completely.

In a bowl, using a fork, mash together the milk or cream and blue cheese. Add the eggs and rice; mix well. Set aside.

Preheat a broiler (griller).

In a 9-inch (23-cm) nonstick flameproof frying pan over medium heat, warm the olive oil. Add the onion and garlic and sauté until soft, about 10 minutes. Add the spinach and salt and pepper to taste and stir until it wilts, about 2 minutes.

Add the egg mixture to the pan holding the spinach and stir together. Cook over medium heat, without stirring, until the eggs are set on the bottom, 2–3 minutes.

Sprinkle the surface with the Parmesan cheese. Slip under the broiler and broil (grill) until puffed and golden, 2–3 minutes. Serve immediately directly from the pan.

Serves 4–6

Summer Succotash

¼ lb (125 g) thickly sliced bacon,
  finely diced
1½ cups (8 oz/250 g) shelled fresh
  lima beans
kernels from 3 ears of corn
  (about 2 cups/12 oz/375 g)
½ lb (250 g) green beans, trimmed and
  cut into 1-inch (2.5-cm) lengths
salt
2 tablespoons unsalted butter
½ cup (4 fl oz/125 ml) milk
½ cup (4 fl oz/125 ml) heavy (double)
  cream
pinch of sugar
freshly ground pepper

When lima beans and sweet corn are ripe from the garden, succotash appears on New England dinner tables. If fresh lima beans are not available, you can use dried lima beans: Soak for a few hours, drain, then simmer in water to cover by 2 inches (5 cm) until not quite tender, about 35 minutes. Add the bacon and cook until the beans are tender, then proceed with the recipe.

*I*n a saucepan, combine the bacon and lima beans with boiling water to cover generously. Cook until the lima beans are almost tender, 15–20 minutes.

Add the corn, green beans and salt to taste and cook until the green beans are tender, 7–10 minutes. Drain and let cool.

In a sauté pan over medium heat, melt the butter. Add the boiled vegetables and cook for 2 minutes.

In a measuring cup, combine the milk and cream. Add ¼ cup (2 fl oz/60 ml) of the milk mixture to the vegetables, along with the sugar and salt and pepper to taste. Simmer over medium-high heat, stirring occasionally, until most of the liquid is gone. Continue adding the milk mixture ¼ cup (2 fl oz/60 ml) at a time and cooking until it is almost gone before adding more liquid. When all the liquid has been absorbed, transfer to a warmed serving dish and serve immediately.

Serves 6

Boston Baked Beans

3 cups (21 oz/660 g) dried small white (navy) beans
¼ lb (125 g) salt pork
4 thin yellow onion slices
⅓ cup (4 oz/125 g) molasses
½ cup (3½ oz/105 g) firmly packed brown sugar
1½ teaspoons salt
½ teaspoon freshly ground pepper
2 teaspoons dry mustard

Three centuries ago in America, the Indians baked beans with local maple syrup and bear fat in handmade clay pots in underground pits. The Pilgrims made their own version of these beans, substituting molasses and salt pork. Thanks to Jean Tenanes, a talented New England cook, for this modern version, which is less sweet and takes less baking time. Serve with warm slices of steamed brown bread.

Pick over and discard any damaged beans or stones. Rinse the beans. Place in a bowl, add plenty of water to cover and soak for about 3 hours.

Drain the beans and place in a saucepan with water to cover by 2 inches (5 cm). Bring to a boil, reduce the heat to low and simmer, uncovered, until almost tender, 25–35 minutes. Drain, reserving the liquid.

Preheat an oven to 300°F (150°C).

Using a sharp knife, cut a crisscross pattern ¼ inch (6 mm) deep in the top of the salt pork. Add to a saucepan of boiling water and boil for 1 minute, then drain.

Spoon the beans into a 2-qt (2-l) baking dish. Top with the salt pork and onion slices. In a saucepan, combine the molasses, brown sugar, salt, pepper, mustard and 1 cup (8 fl oz/250 ml) of the bean cooking liquid. Heat, stirring, to dissolve the sugar. Pour evenly over the beans and add just enough additional bean cooking liquid to cover the beans.

Cover the dish and bake for 4 hours. Remove the cover, scoop up the pork so it rests on top of the beans and continue to bake, uncovered, until the beans are cooked through and caramel-colored and the salt pork is golden, 1½–2 hours longer. If you like, slice the salt pork and serve it alongside.

Serves 6–8

Warm Green Beans and Brown Rice with Sesame Dressing

½ cup (3½ oz/105 g) brown rice
1 cup (8 fl oz/250 ml) chicken or
   vegetable stock (*recipes on page 11*)
   or water
¼ teaspoon salt, plus salt to taste
1 teaspoon Dijon mustard
1 clove garlic, minced
1½ tablespoons rice vinegar or fresh
   lemon juice
2 tablespoons soy sauce
2 teaspoons Asian sesame oil
2 tablespoons corn oil
freshly ground pepper
1¼ lb (625 g) green beans, trimmed
   and cut on the diagonal into 1½-inch
   (4-cm) lengths
1 tablespoon sesame seeds
½ cup (3 oz/90 g) raw peanuts, toasted
   (*see glossary, page 106*)

A very easy dish to make. The flavors are Asian in inspiration. Add a few thin slices of grilled chicken breast to turn it into a light main course.

Rinse the rice well and drain. Place in a heavy saucepan with the stock or water and the ¼ teaspoon salt. Bring to a boil, reduce the heat to low, cover and cook, without stirring, for 45 minutes; do not remove the cover. After 45 minutes, uncover and check to see if the rice is tender and the water is absorbed. If not, re-cover and cook for a few minutes longer until the rice is done. Uncover and fluff the grains with a fork.

Meanwhile, in a small bowl, whisk together the mustard, garlic, vinegar or lemon juice, soy sauce, sesame oil, corn oil and salt and pepper to taste. Set aside.

When the rice is almost ready, fill another saucepan three-fourths full of water and bring to a boil. Add salt to taste and the green beans and cook until just tender, 5–7 minutes.

While the beans are cooking, place the sesame seeds in a small, dry frying pan over medium heat and toast, stirring constantly, until golden, 2–3 minutes. Set aside.

Drain the beans and place in a deep bowl. Immediately add the hot rice, peanuts and the dressing and toss to mix well. Place on a platter, garnish with the toasted sesame seeds and serve at once.

Serves 6

Baked Adzuki Beans with Eggplant and Tomatoes

1 cup (7 oz/220 g) dried adzuki beans
6 fresh parsley stems
pinch of fresh or dried thyme leaves
1 bay leaf
2 small eggplants (aubergines), 1½ lb (750 g) total weight, unpeeled, cut into 1-inch (2.5-cm) cubes
kosher salt
6 tablespoons (3 fl oz/90 ml) olive oil
1 yellow onion, finely chopped
2½ cups (15 oz/470 g) peeled, seeded and chopped tomatoes (fresh or canned)
1 cup (8 fl oz/250 ml) chicken or vegetable stock (recipes on page 11)
½ teaspoon ground allspice
¼ teaspoon red pepper flakes
4 tablespoons fresh basil leaves, shredded
regular salt and freshly ground pepper
½ cup (2 oz/60 g) freshly grated Parmesan cheese

Traditionally made to use up leftovers, this versatile dish is called a tian *in Provence. Any dried beans can be substituted.*

Pick over and discard any damaged beans or stones. Rinse the beans. Place in a bowl, add plenty of water to cover and soak for about 3 hours. Drain the beans and place in a saucepan with water to cover by 2 inches (5 cm). Assemble a bouquet garni: Combine the parsley stems, thyme and bay leaf on a small piece of cheesecloth (muslin), bring the corners together and tie with kitchen string to form a bag. Add to the saucepan. Bring to a boil, reduce the heat to low and simmer, uncovered, until the beans are tender, about 20 minutes. Drain and set aside.

Meanwhile, place the eggplant cubes in a colander and sprinkle with kosher salt. Let drain for 30 minutes. Rinse and pat dry with paper towels.

Preheat an oven to 375°F (190°C). Oil a large baking dish. In a large frying pan over medium-high heat, warm 4 tablespoons (2 fl oz/60 ml) of the olive oil. Add the eggplant and sauté until lightly browned on all sides, 10–15 minutes. Transfer to a dish.

Add the remaining 2 tablespoons olive oil to the pan over medium heat. Add the onion and sauté, stirring, until soft, about 10 minutes. Add the tomatoes and stock and simmer slowly for 5 minutes. Add the eggplant, allspice, red pepper flakes, basil and beans. Season to taste with salt and pepper.

Transfer the mixture to the prepared baking dish. Sprinkle with the Parmesan cheese. Bake until golden brown, about 20 minutes. Serve immediately directly from the dish.

Serves 6

Savory Rice Custard with Roasted Garlic

2 heads garlic

olive oil, as needed

¼ cup (2 fl oz/60 ml) plus 1⅓ cups (11 fl oz/330 ml) water

½ teaspoon salt, plus salt to taste

⅔ cup (5 oz/155 g) short-grain white rice

¼ cup (1½ oz/45 g) minced yellow onion

2 egg yolks, lightly beaten

2 whole eggs, lightly beaten

1 cup (8 fl oz/250 ml) heavy (double) cream

½ teaspoon chopped fresh thyme

½ cup (2 oz/60 g) freshly grated Parmesan cheese

freshly ground pepper

boiling water, as needed

*P*reheat an oven to 350°F (180°C). Remove the excess papery sheaths from the garlic heads and place the garlic in a small baking dish. Drizzle with 1 tablespoon olive oil and the ¼ cup (2 fl oz/60 ml) water. Cover and bake until soft, about 45 minutes. Pass the heads through a food mill or potato ricer to extract the pulp; discard the skins and set the pulp aside. Alternatively, separate into cloves and squeeze the pulp from the skins by hand.

Meanwhile, in a saucepan, bring the 1⅓ cups (11 fl oz/330 ml) water and the ½ teaspoon salt to a boil. Slowly add the rice, reduce the heat to low, cover and cook, without stirring, for 20 minutes; do not remove the cover. After 20 minutes, uncover and check to see if the rice is tender and the water is absorbed. If not, re-cover and cook for a few minutes longer until the rice is done. Remove from the heat, fluff the grains with a fork and place in a bowl to cool.

In a frying pan over medium heat, warm 1½ teaspoons olive oil. Add the onion and sauté, stirring, until soft, about 10 minutes. Transfer to a bowl and add the garlic, cooled rice, egg yolks, whole eggs, cream, thyme, cheese and salt and pepper to taste; mix well.

Oil six ½-cup (4 fl oz/125 ml) ramekins with olive oil. Place them in a larger baking dish. Pour boiling water into the baking dish to reach halfway up the sides of the ramekins. Divide the rice mixture evenly among the ramekins.

Bake until the custards are firm and a knife inserted in the center comes out clean, 30–35 minutes.

Remove the ramekins from the baking dish. Serve hot or warm.

Serves 6

Refried Pinto Beans

1½ cups (10½ oz/330 g) dried red pinto
   beans or red kidney beans
¼ cup (2 oz/60 g) lard, bacon drippings
   or vegetable oil
1 yellow onion, minced
2 fresh serrano or jalapeño peppers,
   seeded (if desired) and minced
4 cloves garlic, minced
1 teaspoon dried oregano
½ teaspoon ground cumin
1 tomato, diced
salt and freshly ground pepper

Refried beans are usually made with a good amount of fat. This version reduces the fat, but is still full of flavor. Garnish with sour cream, sliced avocado and tomato salsa (see black bean soup recipe on page 20 for salsa) or with a mixture of goat cheese, heavy (double) cream and cilantro (fresh coriander).

*P*ick over and discard any damaged beans or stones. Rinse the beans. Place in a bowl, add plenty of water to cover and soak for about 3 hours.

Drain the beans and place in a saucepan with water to cover by 2 inches (5 cm). Bring to a boil, reduce the heat to low and simmer, uncovered, until the skins begin to crack and the beans are very tender, 50–60 minutes. Drain, reserving the liquid.

In a large nonstick frying pan over low heat, warm the lard, bacon drippings or vegetable oil. Add the onion, chili peppers, garlic, oregano and cumin and sauté, stirring, until the onion is very soft, 15 minutes.

Add the tomato, beans and salt and pepper to taste. With the pan still on the heat, mash with a potato masher or wooden spoon until creamy, adding the reserved bean cooking liquid if necessary to achieve the proper consistency.

Transfer to a serving dish and serve.

Serves 6

Spiced Black-eyed Peas with Yogurt and Ginger

1½ cups (10½ oz/330 g) dried
    black-eyed peas
¼ cup (2 fl oz/60 ml) olive oil
2 yellow onions, minced
4 tablespoons minced, peeled fresh
    ginger
6 cloves garlic, minced
1 teaspoon ground coriander
¾ teaspoon ground cumin
¼ teaspoon ground cardamom
2 tomatoes, chopped
½ cup (4 oz/125 g) plain yogurt
salt
¼ teaspoon cayenne pepper
4 tablespoons chopped fresh cilantro
  (fresh coriander)

Here is an ideal side dish for accompanying roasted lemon chicken. Or serve these East Indian–inspired black-eyed peas as a vegetarian main course with steamed basmati rice.

Pick over and discard any damaged peas or stones. Rinse the peas. Place in a bowl, add plenty of water to cover and soak for about 3 hours.

Drain the peas and place in a saucepan with water to cover by 2 inches (5 cm). Bring to a boil, reduce the heat to low and simmer, uncovered, until almost tender, about 35 minutes. Drain the peas, reserving the liquid. Set aside.

In a large frying pan over low heat, warm the olive oil. Add the onions and sauté, stirring, until soft, about 10 minutes. Add the ginger, garlic, coriander, cumin and cardamom and sauté, stirring, for 2 minutes. Add the tomatoes, cover and cook for 2 minutes longer. Uncover and increase the heat to medium. Add 1 tablespoon of the yogurt and continue to stir until it is fully incorporated into the sauce. Continue in the same manner with the remaining yogurt, adding 1 tablespoon at a time.

Add the peas, ½ cup (4 fl oz/125 ml) of the liquid, salt to taste and the cayenne, cover and simmer over medium heat for 15 minutes. Uncover and continue to cook, stirring occasionally, until the liquid is very thick, 3–5 minutes.

Transfer to a platter, garnish with the cilantro and serve.

Serves 6

Peppers Stuffed with Rice, Tomatoes and Corn

1 slice bacon, finely chopped (optional)
½ cup (4 fl oz/125 ml) tomato sauce (recipe on page 12)
1 cup (7 oz/220 g) short-grain white rice
½ teaspoon salt, plus salt to taste
1½ cups (12 fl oz/375 ml) water
kernels from 1 ear of corn, boiled for 1 minute and drained
3 tablespoons chopped fresh basil
freshly ground pepper
6 small red bell peppers (capsicums)
1 cup (8 fl oz/250 ml) chicken or vegetable stock (recipes on page 11) or water

To create a golden crust, sprinkle the stuffed red peppers with fresh bread crumbs and dot with butter before baking. Yellow or green bell peppers, or an assortment, can be substituted for the red peppers. To top with a flavorful sauce, thin garlic mayonnaise (recipe on page 13) with water and spoon over the peppers.

*I*n a frying pan over medium heat, sauté the bacon (if using), stirring, until lightly golden. Add the tomato sauce, rice, the ½ teaspoon salt and the water. Bring to a boil, reduce the heat to low, cover and cook, without stirring, until the rice is almost tender, 15–20 minutes. Remove from the heat and let cool. Mix in the corn kernels, basil and salt and pepper to taste.

Preheat an oven to 375°F (190°C).

Cut off the tops from the peppers and remove and discard the seeds and ribs. In a saucepan large enough to hold the bell peppers, bring the stock or water to a boil. Place the peppers in the stock and simmer for 3 minutes. Drain, reserving the stock.

Fill the peppers with the cooled rice mixture. Stand them in a baking dish in which they fit close together. Pour the reserved stock into the dish and cover with aluminum foil. Bake for 15 minutes. Remove the foil and continue to bake until the rice is tender, about 15 minutes longer.

Transfer to a platter; serve hot or at room temperature.

Serves 6

Wild and White Rice Pilaf with Leeks and Walnuts

2 leeks
3 tablespoons unsalted butter
½ cup (3 oz/90 g) wild rice
3 cups (24 fl oz/750 ml) chicken or vegetable stock *(recipes on page 11)*
¾ teaspoon salt
¾ cup (5 oz/155 g) long-grain white rice
½ cup (2 oz/60 g) walnut pieces, toasted *(see glossary, page 106)*
freshly ground pepper
2 tablespoons chopped fresh chives

A favorite garnish for this dish is fried leeks. To make them, carefully wash 2 leeks, then slice them into very thin strips about 2 inches (5 cm) long. In a deep frying pan, pour in peanut or corn oil to a depth of 1 inch (2.5 cm) and heat to 375°F (190°C). Deep-fry the leeks until golden. Using a slotted spoon, transfer to paper towels to drain.

Cut the leeks, including 2 inches (5 cm) of the tender green, into ½-inch (12-mm) dice. Rinse the diced leeks and dry well. In a saucepan over medium heat, melt the butter. Add the leeks and sauté, stirring, until soft, about 10 minutes.

Meanwhile, rinse the wild rice well and drain. Add to the leeks and stir for 1 minute. Add the stock and salt and bring to a boil. Reduce the heat to low, cover and cook for 25 minutes. Uncover, add the white rice and stir once. Re-cover and continue to cook, without stirring, for 20 minutes; do not remove the cover. After 20 minutes, uncover and check to see if the rice is tender and the water is absorbed. If not, re-cover and cook for a few minutes longer until the rice is done.

Add the walnuts and pepper to taste to the rice and toss to mix well. Transfer to a warmed platter and garnish with the chives and, if desired, fried leeks (see note above). Serve immediately.

Serves 6

Glossary

The following glossary defines terms both generally and specifically as they relate to beans and rice and their preparation. Included are major and unusual ingredients and basic techniques.

ALLSPICE
Sweet spice of Caribbean origin with a flavor suggesting a blend of cinnamon, cloves and nutmeg, hence its name. May be purchased as whole dried berries or ground. When using whole berries, they may be bruised—gently crushed with the bottom of a pan or other heavy instrument—to release more of their flavor.

BARLEY, PEARL
Whole kernels of the mild-tasting grain that are polished 4 to 6 times during processing, resulting in a smooth surface and lustrous gray finish resembling a pearl. Available in most food markets and natural-foods stores.

BAY LEAVES
Dried whole leaves of the bay laurel tree. Pungent and spicy, they flavor simmered dishes, marinades and pickling mixtures. The French variety, sometimes available in specialty-food shops, has a milder, sweeter flavor than California bay leaves. Discard the leaves before serving.

BEL PAESE
Soft-textured, delicately flavored, pale yellow Italian whole-milk cheese.

BELL PEPPER
Fresh, sweet-fleshed, bell-shaped member of the pepper family. Also known as capsicum. Most common in the unripe green form, although ripened red or yellow varieties are also available. Creamy pale yellow, orange and purple-black types can also be found.

To prepare a raw bell pepper, cut it in half lengthwise with a sharp knife. Pull out the stem section from each half, along with the cluster of seeds attached to it. Remove any remaining seeds, along with any thin white membranes, or ribs, to which they are attached. Cut the pepper halves into quarters, strips, thin slices or dice, as called for in the specific recipe.

BLUE CHEESE
Blue-veined cheeses of many varieties have rich, tangy flavors and creamy to crumbly consistencies. Those used in this book include Roquefort, a French cheese made from sheep's milk, with a creamy consistency and a rich, sharp taste; Gorgonzola, a semisoft Italian variety; and Maytag blue, an American blue cheese, generally milder than its European counterparts and with a fairly firm consistency.

BREAD CRUMBS
Fresh or dried bread crumbs are sometimes used to add body and texture or a crisp topping to bean or rice dishes. To make bread crumbs, choose a good-quality, rustic-style loaf made of unbleached wheat flour, with a firm, coarse-textured crumb. For fresh crumbs, cut away the crusts and crumble the bread by hand or in a blender or food processor fitted with the metal blade. For dried crumbs, spread the crumbs on a baking pan. Dry slowly, about 1 hour, in an oven set at its lowest temperature. Fine-textured dried bread crumbs are also sold prepackaged in food markets.

CARDAMOM
Sweet, exotic-tasting spice mainly used in Middle Eastern and Indian cooking and in Scandinavian baking.

CHILI PEPPERS
Any of a wide variety of peppers prized for the mild-to-hot spiciness they impart as a seasoning. Red, ripe chilies are sold fresh and dried. Fresh green chilies include the mild-to-hot, dark green poblano, which resembles a tapered, triangular bell pepper; the long, mild Anaheim (New Mexican); the small, wide, thick-fleshed and fiery jalapeño; and the small, slender, very hot serrano.

For use as a seasoning, fresh chilies are usually cut in halves lengthwise. Then their stems, fiery seeds and white ribs are cut out (below) before the flesh is thinly sliced or finely chopped.

When handling chilies, wear kitchen gloves to prevent any cuts or abrasions on your hands from contacting the pepper's volatile oils; wash your hands well with warm, soapy water, and take special care not to touch your eyes or any other sensitive areas.

CAYENNE PEPPER
Very hot ground spice derived from dried cayenne chili peppers.

CHILI POWDER
Commercial blend of spices featuring ground dried **chili peppers** along with such other seasonings as **cumin**, oregano, cloves, **coriander**, pepper and salt.

CILANTRO
Green, leafy herb resembling flat-leaf (Italian) **parsley**, with a sharp, aromatic, somewhat astringent flavor. Popular in Latin American and Asian cuisines. Also called fresh coriander and commonly referred to as Chinese parsley.

CORIANDER
Small, spicy-sweet seeds of the coriander plant, which is also called **cilantro** or Chinese parsley. Used whole or ground as a seasoning, particularly in Middle Eastern and Indian cuisines.

CORN
Before use, fresh sweet corn must be stripped of its green outer husks and the fine inner silky threads must be removed.

If a recipe calls for removing the raw kernels from an ear of corn, hold the ear by its pointed end, steadying its stalk end on a cutting board. Use a sharp, sturdy knife to cut down and away from you along the ear, stripping off the kernels. Continue turning the ear with each cut.

CORNISH GAME HEN
Small hybrid bird that usually yields a single serving. Although sometimes available fresh, they are most often found in the freezer section of food markets.

CREAM, HEAVY
Cream with a butterfat content of at least 36 percent. For the best flavor and cooking properties, purchase 100 percent natural fresh cream with a short shelf life printed on the carton; avoid long-lasting varieties that have been processed by ultraheat methods. In Britain, use double cream.

CUMIN
Middle Eastern spice with a strong, dusky, aromatic flavor, popular in cuisines of its region of origin along with those of Latin America, India and parts of Europe. Sold either ground or as whole, small, crescent-shaped seeds.

FENNEL
Crisp, refreshing, mildly anise-flavored bulb vegetable, sometimes called by its Italian name, *finocchio*.

FETA CHEESE
Crumbly textured Greek-style cheese made from goat's or sheep's milk, notable for its salty, slightly sharp flavor.

FISH, SMOKED FILLETS
Delicately or more strongly scented with the smoke of the aromatic woods with which they are cured, a wide range of smoked fish—including salmon, trout, herring, mackerel and cod—can be found in the refrigerated counters of delicatessens and well-stocked food stores.

GUACAMOLE
A popular dip or garnish in Mexico and the southwestern United States, made by mashing

GINGER
The rhizome of the tropical ginger plant, which yields a sweet, strong-flavored spice. Whole ginger rhizomes, commonly but mistakenly called roots, can be purchased fresh in a food store or vegetable market.

Before slicing, chopping or grating, the rhizome's brown, papery skin is usually peeled away from the amount being used.

The ginger may then be sliced or chopped with a small paring knife or a chef's knife, or grated against the fine holes of a small grater (shown here).

together ripe avocado, lemon or lime juice and salt, along with such other ingredients as chopped onion, **chili peppers, cilantro** (fresh coriander) and tomato.

HAM HOCK
The narrow ankle section cut from a ham, often used in bean dishes to lend a smoky flavor.

HOT-PEPPER SAUCE
Bottled commercial cooking and table sauce made from fresh or dried hot red **chili peppers.** Many varieties are available, but Tabasco is the most commonly known brand.

LEEKS
Sweet, moderately flavored member of the onion family, long and cylindrical in shape with a pale white root end and dark green leaves. Select firm, unblemished leeks, small to medium in size. Grown in sandy soil, the leafy-topped, multilayered vegetables require thorough cleaning.

MOLASSES
Thick, robust-tasting, syrupy sugarcane by-product of sugar refining. Light molasses results from the first boiling of the syrup; dark molasses from the second boiling.

MONTEREY JACK CHEESE
Semisoft white melting cheese with a mild flavor and buttery texture.

MOZZARELLA
Rindless white, mild-tasting Italian variety of cheese traditionally made from water buffalo's milk and sold fresh. Commercially produced and packaged cow's milk mozzarella is now much more common, although it has less flavor. Look for fresh mozzarella sold immersed in water. Mozzarella is also sometimes smoked, yielding a firmer textured, aromatic but still mild cheese.

MUSHROOMS
With their meaty textures and rich, earthy flavors, mushrooms are used to enrich many bean and rice dishes. Cultivated white and brown mushrooms are widely available in food markets and greengrocers. Chanterelles, subtly flavored, usually pale yellow,

EGGS, SEPARATING

To separate an egg, crack the shell in half by tapping it against the side of a bowl and then breaking it apart with your fingers. Holding the shell halves over the bowl, gently transfer the whole yolk back and forth between them, letting the clear white drop away into the bowl, as shown below.

Take care not to cut into the yolk with the edges of the shell (the whites will not beat properly if they contain any yolk). Transfer the yolk to another bowl.

Alternatively, gently pour the egg from the shell onto the slightly cupped fingers of your outstretched (clean) hand, held over a bowl. Let the whites fall between your fingers into the bowl; the whole yolk will remain in your hand. The same basic function is also performed by an aluminum, ceramic or plastic egg separator placed over a bowl. The separator holds the yolk intact in its cuplike center while allowing the white to drip out through one or more slots in its side into the bowl.

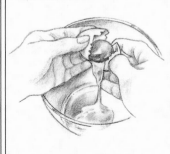

trumpet-shaped wild mushrooms about 2–3 inches (5–7.5 cm) in length, are also cultivated commercially. Shiitakes, meaty-flavored Asian mushrooms, have flat, dark brown caps usually 2–3 inches (5–7.5 cm) in diameter and are available fresh with increasing frequency, particularly in Asian food shops. They are also sold dried, requiring soaking in warm water to cover for approximately 20 minutes before use. Porcini, a widely used Italian term for *Boletus edulis* and also known by the French term *cèpes,* are popular wild mushrooms with a rich, meaty flavor. Most commonly sold in dried form in Italian delicatessens and specialty-food shops, they are reconstituted in liquid as a flavoring for soups, stews, sauces and stuffings.

MUSTARD
Mustard is available in three forms: whole seeds; powdered, referred to as dry mustard; and prepared, which is made from powdered or coarsely ground mustard seed mixed with liquid such as vinegar or wine. Hot, spicy Dijon mustard is made in Dijon, France, from powdered dark brown mustard seeds (unless otherwise marked *blanc*) and white wine or wine vinegar. Pale in color, fairly hot and sharp tasting, true Dijon mustard and non-French blends labeled "Dijon-style" are widely available in most food markets and specialty-food stores. Dry mustard is an intensely hot powder ground from mustard seeds.

NUTS, TOASTING
Toasting brings out the full flavor and aroma of nuts. To toast most nuts, preheat an oven to 325°F (165°C). Spread the nuts in a single layer on a baking sheet and toast in the oven until they just begin to change color, 5–10 minutes. Remove from the oven and let cool to room temperature.

It is best to toast pine nuts on the stove top, because they are delicate and require constant attention. Place in a dry, small frying pan over medium-low heat and toast, shaking the pan constantly, until golden.

ONIONS
A host of onions is used to enhance the flavor of bean and rice dishes. Green onions, also called spring onions or scallions, are a variety harvested immature, leaves and all, before their bulbs have formed. The green and white parts may both be enjoyed, raw or cooked, for their mild but still pronounced onion flavor. Red (Spanish) onions are a mild, sweet variety of onion with purplish red skin and red-tinged white flesh.

White-skinned, white-fleshed onions tend to be sweet and mild. Yellow onions are the common, white-fleshed, strong-flavored variety distinguished by their dry, yellowish brown skins. Small but pungent pearl onions about ¾ inch (2 cm) in diameter, also known as pickling onions, are sometimes added whole to recipes.

PANCETTA
Italian-style unsmoked bacon cured with salt and pepper. May be sold flat or rolled into a large sausage shape. Available in Italian delicatessens and specialty-food stores.

PAPRIKA
Powdered spice derived from the dried paprika pepper; popular in several European cuisines and available in sweet, mild and hot forms.

PARSLEY
This widely used fresh herb is available in two varieties: the more popular curly-leaf type and a flat-leaf type, also known as Italian parsley.

OILS
Oils not only provide a medium in which foods may be browned without sticking, but can also subtly enhance the flavor of recipes in which they are used. Store all oils in airtight containers away from heat and light.

Extra-virgin olive oil, extracted from olives on the first pressing without use of heat or chemicals, is prized for its pure, fruity taste and golden to pale green hue. Many brands, varying in color and strength of flavor, are now widely available; choose one that suits your taste. The higher-priced extra-virgin olive oils usually are of better quality. Products labeled **pure olive oil,** less aromatic and flavorful, may be used for all-purpose cooking.

Pale gold **peanut oil** has a subtle hint of the peanut's richness.

Rich, flavorful and aromatic *sesame oil* is pressed from sesame seeds. Sesame oils from China and Japan are made with toasted sesame seeds, resulting in a dark, strong oil used as a flavoring ingredient; their low smoking temperature makes them unsuitable for using alone for cooking. Cold-pressed sesame oil, made from untoasted seeds, is lighter in color and taste, and may be used for cooking.

Walnut oil, popular in dressings and as a seasoning, conveys the rich taste of the nuts from which it is pressed; seek out oil made from lightly toasted nuts, which has a full but not too assertive flavor.

Flavorless *vegetable* and seed oils such as *safflower* and *corn oil* are employed for their high cooking temperatures and bland flavor.

PEAS

Sweet garden peas, freshly shelled from their tough pods, are one of early summer's great delicacies; at other times of year, frozen peas—particularly the small variety labeled *petite peas*—are an acceptable substitute. Two related types of pea require no shelling, and are eaten pods and all. Snow peas, also known as Chinese pea pods or by the French *mangetout*—"eat it all"—are flat pods containing tiny, immature peas. Larger pods may require stringing before cooking; tear off the strings in the same motion with which the stem ends are snapped off by hand. Plump sugar snap peas are a cross between garden peas and snow peas; some require stringing, while other varieties are stringless.

Sugar Snap Peas

Snow Peas

PECORINO CHEESE

Italian sheep's milk cheese, sold either fresh or aged. Two of its most popular aged forms are pecorino romano and pecorino sardo; the latter cheese is tangier than the former.

PINE NUTS

Small, ivory-colored seeds extracted from the cones of a species of pine tree, with a rich, slightly resinous flavor.

RED PEPPER FLAKES

Coarsely ground flakes of dried red **chili peppers,** including seeds, which add moderately hot flavor to the foods they season.

SAFFRON

Intensely aromatic, golden orange spice made from the dried stigmas of a species of crocus; used to perfume and color many classic Mediterranean and East Indian dishes. Sold either as threads—the dried stigmas—or in powdered form. Look for products labeled pure saffron.

SALT, KOSHER

Coarse-grained salt with no additives and a less salty taste than table salt.

SALT PORK

A form of salt-cured slab bacon consisting largely of pork fat, used as an enrichment and seasoning in a wide range of traditional savory dishes, including baked beans. Available in good butcher shops and the meat departments of well-stocked food stores.

SAVORY, SUMMER

Delicate green herb that complements the flavors of vegetables, seafood and poultry. Best in its fresh form, although also widely available dried.

SCALLOPS

Bivalve mollusks that come in two common varieties: the round flesh of sea scallops is usually 1½ inches (4 cm) in diameter, while the bay scallop is considerably smaller. Usually sold already shelled.

STOCK

Flavorful liquid derived from slowly simmering chicken, meat, fish or vegetables in water, along with herbs and aromatic vegetables. Used as the primary cooking liquid or moistening and flavoring agent in many recipes. Stock can be made fairly easily at home, to be frozen for future use. Many good-quality canned stocks or broths, in regular or concentrated form, are also available; they tend to be saltier than homemade stock, so recipes in which they are used should be carefully tasted for seasoning. Excellent stocks can also be found in the freezer section of quality food stores.

TAHINI

Smooth, rich paste ground from sesame seeds and used in Middle Eastern cooking to enrich the flavor and texture of both savory and sweet dishes. Jars and cans of tahini can be found in ethnic markets and well-stocked food stores.

THYME

Fragrant, clean-tasting, small-leaved herb popular fresh or dried as a seasoning for poultry, light meats, seafood or vegetables.

TOMATOES

During summer, when tomatoes are in season, use the best sun-ripened tomatoes you can find. At other times of year, plum tomatoes, sometimes called Roma or egg tomatoes, are likely to have the best flavor and texture; for cooking, canned whole plum tomatoes are also good. Small cherry tomatoes, barely bigger than the fruit after which they are descriptively named, also have a pronounced flavor that makes them ideal candidates for use during their peak summer season.

To peel fresh tomatoes, first bring a saucepan of water to a boil. Using a small, sharp knife, cut out the core from the stem end of the tomato. Then cut a shallow X in the skin at the tomato's base. Submerge for about 20 seconds in the boiling water, then remove and dip in a bowl of cold water. Starting at the X, peel the skin from the tomato, using your fingertips and, if necessary, the knife blade. Cut the tomatoes in half and turn each half cut-side down. Then cut as directed in individual recipes.

To seed a tomato, cut it in half crosswise. Squeeze gently to force out the seed sacks.

TURMERIC

Pungent, earthy-flavored ground spice that, like **saffron,** adds a vibrant yellow color to any dish.

VINEGARS

Literally "sour" wine, vinegar results when certain strains of yeast cause wine—or some other alcoholic liquid such as apple cider or Japanese rice wine—to ferment for a second time, turning it acidic. The best-quality wine vinegars begin with good-quality wine. Red wine vinegar, like the wine from which it is made, has a more robust flavor than vinegar produced from white wine. Champagne vinegar is prized for its delicate flavor. Balsamic vinegar, a specialty of Modena, Italy, is made from reduced grape juice and aged for many years. Flavored vinegars are made by adding herbs such as tarragon and dill or fruits such as raspberries.

Index

ACKNOWLEDGMENTS

The publishers would like to thank the following people and organizations for their generous assistance and support in producing this book:
Anita Anderson, Jean Sears Tenanes, Sharon C. Lott, Stephen W. Griswold, Ken DellaPenta, Jennifer Mullins, Jennifer Hauser, Tarji Mickelson,
the buyers for Gardener's Eden, and the buyers and store managers for Hold Everything, Pottery Barn and Williams-Sonoma stores.

The following kindly lent props for the photography:
Biordi Art Imports, Candelier, Fillamento, Fredericksen Hardware, J. Goldsmith Antiques,
Sue Fisher King, Lorraine Puckett, RH, and Chuck Williams.